ACCIDENTS IN NORTH AMERICAN MOUNTAINEERING

VOLUME 7 • NUMBER 5 • ISSUE 53

2000

THE AMERICAN ALPINE CLUB
GOLDEN

THE ALPINE CLUB OF CANADA
BANFF

ISSN   0065-082X

ISBN   0-930410-88-2

Manufactured in the United States of America

Published by
The American Alpine Club, Inc.
710 Tenth Street, Suite 100
Golden, CO 80401

Cover
The cover photograph, by Colt Landreth, is of the Gendarme on Bugaboo Spire, taken with a Leica Minilux with Fuji Velvia film.

The back cover photograph, taken from Chasm View by Bill May, is of Lamb's Slide on the East Face of Longs Peak. There have been about 75 accidents on this route since Reverend Lamb began the trend.

♲ Printed on recycled paper

CONTENTS

EDITORIAL 1

ACCIDENTS AND ANALYSES 3

    Canada 3

    United States 17

STATISTICAL TABLES 83

MOUNTAIN RESCUE UNITS IN NORTH AMERICA 88

MOUNTAIN RESCUE ASSOCIATION OFFICERS 92

SAFETY COMMITTEES 1999

The American Alpine Club

Aram Attarian, John Dill, Mike Gauthier, Daryl Miller, Jeff Sheetz, James Yester, and John E. (Jed) Williamson *(Chairman)*

The Alpine Club of Canada

Helmut Microys, Murray Toft, and Rod Plasman *(Chairman)*

ACCIDENTS IN
NORTH AMERICAN MOUNTAINEERING
Fifty-Third Annual Report of the Safety Committees
of The American Alpine Club and The Alpine Club of Canada

Canada: Many thanks to Rod Plasman for compiling last year's accident information.

The number of accidents that occurred in 1999 was average in comparison to previous years. There was a noticeable increase in the number of accidents that occurred while individuals were either climbing alone or climbing unroped. The consequences of these accidents were severe—three deaths, some amputated fingers, and one person with both legs broken. There was also a marked increase in the number of accidents that occurred on snow and ice. This could possibly be attributed to the poor conditions found on many alpine climbs due to the generally cold and wet summer in western Canada.

There was one fatal rock climbing accident that occurred as a result of the climbers going off route. Climbers should note that guidebooks can quickly become outdated when bolt belays replace natural or piton belays. If the new belay is placed five meters to one side of the original, suddenly the directions "go up and right from the belay" can take on a whole new meaning.

There were no accidents reported from the St. Elias area in the Yukon, even though it was one of their busiest seasons on record (46 climbing expeditions with 176 people in total). Poor weather and cold temperatures were reported, so perhaps some of these parties spent more time in their tent than they did climbing.

Thank you to the following people who contributed to the Canadian section of this year's book: Marc Ledwidge, Sylvia Forest, George Field, Lloyd Freese, Ron Harris, Larry Stanier, Derek Holtved, Deborah Boulton, David Henderson, Scott Larson, Darlene Snider, Linda Hillard, Bruce Godlien, Doug Fulford, Jim Racette, Chris Perry, Peter Staszelis, Bonnie Hamilton and the staff at Mount Robson Provincial Park Ranger office.

United States: This was a big year for the category "other" in terms of causes for accidents. There were many variations on familiar themes. Rappel/lowering problems abounded, including short ropes and Gri-Gri brake devices not being understood. There was one accident involving a Gri-Gri that could not be reported on in detail. A climber fell 45 meters to his death in Tettegouche State Park (MN) when the lowering system failed. Any time there is the possibility that equipment may have been part of the cause, we try to include a narrative report. If useful information is forthcoming, we will include it next year.

Most of the "falling rock" problems this year were due to rocks breaking loose when stepped on or grabbed. Some of these may have been prevented by better testing of holds, but most seemed to be a geology problem, including the lack of the climbers understanding the nature of the rock formation. There were a number of "unable to self-arrest" incidents, often accompanied by misuse of crampons; i.e., wearing crampons when conditions warranted not doing so.

We try to include comments from one or two major climbing areas in this introduction. This year, Jim Detterline, a Longs Peak Ranger, said there were a total of 208 search, rescue, medical, and fatality incidents to which they responded. He pointed out that climbers comprised only 10 percent of these incidents, and he indicated this to be normal and consistent with annual Rocky Mountain National Park climbing accidents. His data reveal that the average is 12 percent over the past 20 years. While there were no climbing fatalities, there were three hiker and two lightning strike deaths.

An important change noted by Detterline is that the Northcutt-Carter Route on Hallett Peak experienced a major rockslide, turning into a 5.11 climb now. He concluded by saying that the rescues needed were generally accomplished with short, inexpensive missions.

Reports were received from some places we have not heard from in a long time, as well as from some new sites. Unfortunately, there were several locations from whom we did not receive information. These include Arizona, Montana, New Hampshire, Devil's Tower, Devil's Lake State Park, Zion National Park, Smith Rocks, and Salt Lake City. Still, it is unlikely that climbing fatalities or many serious injuries occurred in these places, because these incidents tend to get forwarded by AAC members who find reports in local newspapers.

In addition to the Safety Committee, we are grateful to the following—with apologies for any omissions—for collecting data and helping with the report: Hank Alicandri, Micki Canfield, Jim Detterline, Renny Jackson, Bill May, Leo Paik, Robert Speik, all individuals who sent personal stories in, and, of course, George Sainsbury.

John E. (Jed) Williamson
Managing Editor
7 River Ridge Road
Hanover, NH 03755
e-mail: jedwmsn@sover.net

Nancy Hansen
Canadian Editor
Box 8040
Canmore, Alberta T1W 2T8
e-mail: nhansen@telusplanet.net

CANADA

FALLING ICE, POOR POSITION
Alberta, Banff National Park, Mount Wilson, Ice Nine

On January 24 a party of three had begun the first of pitch Ice Nine, a water ice Grade 6 route. One climber was leading, one was belaying from behind the curtain of the first pitch and the third climber was sitting on her pack watching the leader climb. When the leader was about ten meters up the pitch, a large hanging piece to the right of the route fell. It is estimated that this piece was about 36 cubic meters. The piece missed the belayer but hit the climber who was watching the leader. The main piece of ice hardly broke up and buried the climber under one meter of ice. She sustained severe crushing injuries. The two other climbers were unable to dig her out. They reached the highway in about ten minutes and flagged down a park snowplow operator who reported the incident to park dispatch immediately. Warden service rescue crews responded by ground and helicopter. It took over an hour to dig the victim out from under the solid ice using pneumatic hammers and picks.

Analysis
Falling ice is a major objective hazard in waterfall ice climbing. Overnight temperatures had been –25° C. However, it was a sunny day and the southern exposure of the route resulted in significant radiation effect. Unfortunately, the victim was standing directly underneath the hanging ice curtain. (Source: Parks Canada Warden Service)

OFF ROUTE, INADEQUATE EQUIPMENT, CLIMBING ALONE, WEATHER, INEXPERIENCE
Alberta, Jasper National Park, Columbia Icefield, Mount Snowdome

J.R. (28) hitchhiked to the Columbia Icefields on February 20, and hiked to the base of the difficult and hazardous alpine ice route "Slipstream" later that day. At 0400 on February 21, J.R. started climbing. Conditions were good, and he reached the top of the route four or five hours later. Although he started the climb in good weather, when he reached the top, he was in a blizzard. Because he was climbing alone, he had planned on taking a rarely used descent route which avoided the heavily crevassed areas of the normal descent. Poor weather and darkness prevented him from finding the correct gully. He tried several gullies only to discover that he was at the top of cliffs too high for his rappel rope. Since J.R. had no bivouac gear or stove, he continued moving all night. At some point during his many ascents and descents, J.R. realized that his hands were badly frostbitten from holding the metal ice tools with soggy mitts. On the morning of February 22, he found a gully that brought him down to the Athabasca Glacier and he hiked out to the highway by 1600 hours. He then flagged down a passing motorist and was driven to the Mineral Springs Hospital in Banff. J.R. was treated for frostbite to all 10 fingers and other parts of his hands. He eventually had to get several of his finger tips amputated due to the severe frostbite.

In the meantime, J.R. was reported overdue by his roommate at 1000 on February 22. Details were sketchy about his destination; all that R.P. knew was that his roommate had gone to the Icefields, and possibly to Mt. Snowdome. Upon further investigation, it was determined that J.R. was likely attempting Slipstream. J.R. left a note with R.P., saying that if he was not back on Monday that something had gone wrong. J.R. was a very skilled ice climber with minimal winter mountaineering experience.

Wardens initiated an investigation, which included a ground search party skiing towards the base of Slipstream, and a helicopter response. The search party found no evidence of human activity, however visibility was poor due to high winds, blowing snow and obscured skies. The helicopter was on standby waiting for suitable flying conditions. By 1700, the helicopter was still grounded. At 0200 on February 23, R.P. called wardens to inform them J.R. had returned home, and was in the hospital with frostbite.

Analysis
Soloing has become increasingly popular, but there are several hazards that go along with it, aside from the obvious lack of belay capabilities. Most notably, the summit of Snowdome, as well as the lower glaciers, is riddled with crevasses, making unroped travel hazardous. The probability of staying healthy on the Columbia Icefields in bad weather with no bivouac gear is considerably reduced when alone. (Source: Parks Canada Warden Service, victim)

FALLING ICE, FALL ON ICE
Alberta, Banff National Park, Mount Wilson, Oh Le Tabernac
On March 17 the lead climber of a party of two was ten meters up the first pitch of Oh Le Tabernac, a water ice Grade 5+ route. He was just above his second screw when he heard a cracking noise. He told his belayer about it just as the ice he was standing on broke free. A ten by three-meter piece broke off and he crashed to the ground sustaining multiple fractures and serious head trauma. His partner stabilized him and ran to the road to get help. He was evacuated by heli-sling by a warden service rescue crew, flown to the Banff hospital, and then flown to Calgary. He died a few days later from his injuries.

Analysis
This route usually has a horizontal crack across it due to the detached nature of the pillar. Although many climbers comment on this feature, this is the first serious accident resulting from it. It is unclear how much ice fell on the victim, but given his injuries, it is likely that he was hit by the large piece which broke free. (Source: Parks Canada Warden Service)

CORNICE FAILURE
Alberta, Jasper National Park, Columbia Icefield, Mount Andromeda
At approximately 0230 on May 30, two climbers (22 and 23) departed the climbers' parking lot to ascend the Skyladder route on Mount Andromeda. Later that morning, they overtook another climbing party of three from Seattle near

the top of the route and proceeded along the summit ridge towards the summit of Mt. Andromeda. The pair was last seen by the Seattle climbers some distance above them, standing near a cornice. Some time later, when the Seattle climbers looked up again, the pair were gone from view. Their tracks were obliterated by blowing snow, so it was not clear whether the climbers had pushed on quickly to the summit. However the Seattle climbers reported the incident later that day in the event that something had gone wrong.

Park wardens initiated an investigation, but were limited by high winds and poor visibility. On the morning of May 31, the weather had improved enough for a flight over the area, and wardens immediately spotted two persons near the bottom of the Northwest Shoulder Direct route, on the glacier. Despite high winds, wardens were able to sling to within half a kilometer of the victims. Both climbers were deceased, after having fallen 550 meters down a near vertical rock face.

Analysis

In reconstructing the likely cause of the accident, wardens believe that the two climbers were standing too close to a cornice on the summit ridge of Mount Andromeda, either together, or close enough that one pulled the other off when the cornice failed under their weight. (Source: Parks Canada Warden Service)

PROTECTION PULLED, OFF ROUTE
Alberta, Ha Ling Peak (formerly known as Chinaman's Peak)

On July 6, two climbers set out on the Northeast Ridge of Ha Ling Peak (5.6/ 5.7). The climbers got off route on the third or fourth pitch, and discovered by the sixth pitch that the climbing was much more difficult than 5.7, the protection was next to none, and the rock was loose. The lead climber decided to retreat and attempted to be lowered from a Friend placed in a shallow crack. While being lowered, both of his pieces of protection pulled out and he fell past his belayer for a total of approximately 80 meters.

The belayer, J.S., lowered to his partner, and found him conscious; however, he soon lost consciousness and stopped breathing. J.S. performed artificial respiration, but soon left to call for help. J.S. reported the incident to some other climbers, and then returned to the base of the third pitch (the victim was hanging between the third and fourth pitches). Kananaskis Emergency Services personnel were slung in and removed J.S. in a screamer suit. The victim was pronounced dead, lowered to the base of the third pitch and heli-slung off the mountain. (Source: Kananaskis Country Alpine Specialist)

Analysis

Both climbers were quite experienced. However, many climbers, both experienced and not so experienced have gone off route on the Northeast Ridge of Ha Ling. The climbers did not have pitons or a hammer with them. Properly placed pitons (if it were possible) may have made a much safer anchor than one Friend placed in a shallow crack. (Source: Nancy Hansen)

WEATHER, INADEQUATE EQUIPMENT, INEXPERIENCE
Alberta, Jasper National Park, Mounts Charlton and Unwin

On July 15, two inexperienced climbers (both 25) climbed Mount Charlton in the company of two American climbers whom they met on the mountain. In late afternoon, in deteriorating weather, the inexperienced pair continued from the Charlton-Unwin Col up the East Ridge of Mount Unwin towards its summit while the American climbers returned to their bivouac site. The inexperienced pair were soon engulfed in a whiteout and became disoriented and lost. They wandered around the upper mountain over numerous crevasses and to the edge of the large icefall on the North Face. Finally, they bivouacked in a shallow snow cave on Unwins' East Ridge. The whiteout continued the next day, and the subjects became even more disoriented. They had minimal clothing, minimal food, and no water. They built a second snow cave below the summit of Mount Unwin on the North Ridge/Face, and as they prepared for another night out, they were spotted and evacuated by helicopter.

The two Americans reported the climbers overdue when they did not return to the lower bivouac site. The weather had been very poor for three days previous, with over 40 centimeters of new snow deposited in 48 hours accompanied by high winds. A helicopter search of the mountain revealed several large new avalanches, and tracks on the lower glacier. The upper mountain was obscured in cloud, so a ground party was placed on the glacier to search on foot. The ground party followed tracks to the col, and ascended Unwin to just below its summit while the helicopter continued to search by air. The subjects were spotted by air on the opposite side of the mountain, but due to fluctuating low cloud levels, it was not possible to sling to them. After several unsuccessful attempts to reach the subjects, a warden was slung in to a point below their location. The warden climbed up to the subjects, who were guided down to a lower elevation where sling evacuation was possible.

Analysis

Poor weather, heavy snowfalls, and whiteout conditions are the primary contributing causes of this mishap. The subjects lacked the judgment to turn back when the weather deteriorated, and did not plan for white-out navigation. The col and lower East Ridge of Mount Unwin are very broad, and in poor visibility it is extremely difficult to route find without a map and compass or wands. The Charlton-Unwin massif is large and serious, and is prone to poor weather. It has serious objective hazards on all routes, including icefalls, crevasses, bergschrunds, cornices, and avalanche slopes above and below all routes. It is very easy to get lost on the upper mountain, due to the featureless nature of the terrain. Climbers attempting this massif should get thorough information on routes and hazards, and have adequate navigation and bivouac equipment. (Source: Parks Canada Warden Service)

FALL ON ICE, CLIMBING UNROPED, and STRANDED, INEXPERIENCE
Alberta, Jasper National Park, Columbia Icefield, Mount Athabasca

On July 19, a party of two (both 38) were ascending the Northeast Ridge of

Mount Athabasca, when they encountered technical, exposed terrain. One was hesitant about climbing through this section, so the other climber offered to unrope, solo the difficult section, and drop a top rope down from above. While soloing out onto the south slopes, the climber encountered a thin veneer of ice on the rock. With both crampons and an ice ax in the thin ice, the sheet of ice gave way, and the climber fell approximately 100 meters. He sustained serious injuries to his head and both legs. Both spent the night on the mountain. The uninjured climber anchored himself to the mountain with a snow picket, but was afraid to move from his location. The next morning, with two broken legs, the injured climber crawled over the Boundary–North Glacier Col and made his way down the mountain to a telephone to call for help.

A helicopter was brought over from Golden, and two wardens were slung in to the stranded climber. It was dicey terrain, but the rescuers were able to remain on the heli-sling rope, hike up to the stranded climber and hook him on. All three slung off to the staging area.

Analysis

The route was in poor condition, being plastered in snow and verglas. The rock quality on the lower section of this ridge is extremely poor and is generally avoided by most climbers, who prefer to access the ridge higher up. (Source: Parks Canada Warden Service)

FALL ON ROCK, WRONG ROUTE, INAPPROPRIATE EQUIPMENT
Alberta, Banff National Park, Castle Mountain

On July 27 a party of two began climbing what they thought was the popular Brewers Buttress route, II, 5.6. Unfortunately, they were one buttress too far to the north. On the first pitch, the leader fell about 20 meters with his belayer stopping him one meter above the ground. His highest piece of protection failed but the next one held him and prevented a ground fall. He sustained hand and arm fractures as well as head trauma. His partner was able to call for help with a cell phone. He was evacuated by heli-sling shortly afterwards.

Analysis

The injured climber was planning on using this multi-pitch rock route as "training ground" for alpine routes. He was wearing plastic boots. Most climbers use rock shoes in this terrain. It is fortunate that the one piece of protection held and that his belayer was able to stop him before he hit the ground. One can only speculate what kind of difficulties they may have encountered higher up in this uncharted terrain. (Source: Parks Canada Warden Service)

FALL IN CREVASSE
Alberta, Jasper National Park, Columbia Icefield

At 1840 on August 5, two climbers came off the Columbia Icefield to report that two members of their party of ten were injured and needed helicopter evacuation. All members were Russian Canadian and were planning to travel down the Columbia Glacier icefall from the trench. T.S. (37) was the middle member of a three-person rope team. She lost her balance while crossing a crevasse and fell in seven meters, injuring her head in the fall. M.S. (34), the last person on the rope, attempted to arrest T.S.'s fall, and was pulled into another crevasse. In the process, M.S. caught his crampon and injured his ankle. The remaining members of the group evacuated the fallen climbers from their respective crevasses and assisted them to a location where a helicopter could land.

Wardens flew to the accident site at the trench with a Bell 407 from Golden. The helicopter was able to land at the site, and the victims were loaded into the helicopter and were transported directly to Emergency Medical Services.

Analysis

The Columbia Glacier is an extremely broken icefall, which is difficult to navigate even under ideal circumstances. Falling into a crevasse is almost inevitable when attempting to travel through an icefall of this nature. (Source: Parks Canada Warden Service)

ROCKFALL, POOR POSITION, POOR JUDGMENT
Alberta, Jasper National Park, Mount Edith Cavell

On August 20, two climbers (F 43, M 54) began ascending the North Face route on Mount Edith Cavell. They began at 1500 on a hot day, when rock fall is at its worst. One of the climbers was hit directly on the head by a large rock, knocking her unconscious and causing her to fall approximately 100 meters to the glacier below. The climbers were not roped at the time, but both had helmets on. She was unconscious for about ten minutes. She suffered from amnesia and headaches the rest of the day. The pair bivouacked on the Angel Glacier for the night. The second climber subsequently suffered severe back spasms (a recurring problem) as a result of bivouacking on the cold hard surface, and could not go for help. They spent a second night on the glacier waiting for help to arrive.

The search for the climbers began when their registered check-in time came and went without their reporting in. The decision was made to bring in a helicopter after no evidence of the climbers could be found on the trail or with binoculars. A Bell 407 was brought over from Golden, and the mountain was searched by air. A warden was also dropped at the Verdant Creek/Astoria River trail junction to hike up the West Ridge of Cavell on foot. After an extensive search by air, the overdue climbers were found at their bivouac site low on the Angel Glacier. The helicopter was able to land at their location, and the climbers were evacuated to the staging area.

Analysis

The climbers did not depart the Cavell parking lot until 1000. They found the rock climbing up to the Angel Glacier to be quite tricky and therefore went slowly. They arrived at the base of the North Face route at 1500, and planned to climb the lower part of the route in the late afternoon and to bivouac on the large ledge halfway up the face. The weather was warm, and rock fall at that time of day was extensive. The lower part of this route is subject to a considerable amount of falling rock and ice. The climbers were well prepared and had done extensive research on this route. They had been to the base of the route three times prior to this attempt and were familiar with the terrain. Despite their experience and knowledge, they chose to ascend the most hazardous part of the face in the heat of the afternoon when rockfall is at its worst. This turned out to be a critical judgment error. Luckily both climbers had helmets on, which undoubtedly saved the female climber's life. (Source: Parks Canada Warden Service)

FALL ON ICE, EQUIPMENT FAILURE
Alberta, Banff National Park, Mount Aberdeen

On August 20, L.S. (40) was guiding K.B. (61) on Mount Aberdeen. They reached the toe of the Aberdeen Glacier at approximately 0700. They moved together on a two-meter short-rope up 50 meters of firm snow and started to traverse 25-degree ice to reach a stance at the base of the steeper ice. K.B. slipped and L.S. held his weight easily. While K.B. was regaining his footing, L.S.'s crampon broke and they fell together down the glacier. After sliding for about 30 meters on the rock covered ice, L.S. was able to self arrest and they stopped at a small rock pile. K.B. had fractured and dislocated the head of his humerus and had back pain. After applying first aid to K.B. for several minutes, L.S. realized that he had broken his ulna and dislocated his radius (both lower arm bones) in the initial fall. L.S. was able to call the Banff Park Warden Service through the Lake Louise Ski area and request assistance. The climbers were slung out within the hour.

Analysis

Short-roping on low-angle ice and snow is standard practice amongst Mountain Guides. It is a necessary and effective tool that relies very little on equipment except for the rope, ice ax, and crampons. However, when the equipment fails or the techniques are poorly applied, the results can be catastrophic. In this case the crampons were very high quality (Charlet Moser S12 with heel binding and toe lanyard) but well used. The crampon strap broke on the outside of the guide's left foot. His left leg was braced flat-footed on 25-degree ice to hold his own and the client's weight, so when the strap broke the whole system fell apart. The strap looked like it had been cut, so it is possible it had been damaged while walking through snow covered rocks or while mixed climbing. The use of the radio in an area with an excellent mountain rescue service made the solution to a very difficult situation simple. (Source: L.S.)

FALL ON ROCK, LOOSE ROCK, FATIGUE
Alberta, Banff National Park, Mount Victoria

I (35) was climbing with two friends, H.N. (32) and E.D. (26) on August 28. We departed from the Abbot Pass Hut early Saturday morning to attempt a south to north traverse of Mount Victoria. The weather and conditions were excellent, and we were equipped for a likely bivouac around the north summit. We took a brief break at the main summit at about 1100. We continued on down and north along the ridge where we encountered the first of some very loose though not technically difficult climbing. Following this pitch the difficulties eased and the climbing was mostly fourth-class. We were roped and using running belays. At about 1630 and after a lot of exposed climbing we were nearing the end of the rotten towers on the route. I stepped on a large flat rock, which shifted under my weight. I had to jump back to avoid slipping off the west side of the mountain. I had been leading all day and after the incident realized that I was quite tired and set up a belay just past this point and was joined by my partners. We took a break and I asked H.N. if he could lead from there because I didn't want to make any kind of mistake in the gear placements over the next few pitches. H.N. led off across some steepish terrain that was a mixture of snow and ice, and there was some discussion about whether it was better with or without crampons. E.D. and I decided to wear crampons. Approximately ten meters after the belay, there was a short, steep, very loose down-climb. H.N. was able to place a solid tri-cam at the base of the section, and then another solid midpoint anchor before the easier ground. As I entered this section I turned to face in and gently work myself down through the loose rock and I slipped. It is possible that my crampons skated on the rock, or that the loose rock all collapsed out from under me. The tri-cam was placed horizontally in solid rock and slightly above where I was standing, but was approximately ten to twelve meters away. As a result I took a long pendulum fall, bouncing hard three times before coming to a rest below the tri-cam. During the fall I tried to stop myself and this is what likely resulted in the severe lacerations to both of my hands. Very shaken, I came to rest on a small snowfield. There was a lot of blood coming from my hands. I was belayed on a tight rope to E.D., who was at the midpoint anchor. We bandaged my hands, changed positions on the rope, and I was belayed from both ends across to the leader's station where we debated what to do. As we reassessed my injuries, it became apparent that there was some potential damage to my back and possibly some broken ribs which were becoming more painful by the minute. It was also apparent that my right hand was virtually unusable. As a result we contacted the wardens by cell phone and requested assistance. We were plucked off the ridge approximately an hour later by heli-sling and I was taken to hospital by ambulance. Injuries included at least one rib separated from the cartilage on my right side, severed muscles in my right hand between the thumb and forefinger and a deep laceration in my lower left palm. (Source: victim)

Analysis

It is possible that the fall was caused by the climber wearing crampons in the rocky section. Whether to wear crampons in certain mixed terrain can be a tough decision. In this case, one person had made it through the section without crampons, one had made it with crampons, and the final climber was unlucky. (Source: Parks Canada Warden Service, Nancy Hansen)

FALL ON ROCK, HANDHOLD PULLED
Alberta, Mount Laurie (Yamnuska)

On September 17, C.H. and C.S. were climbing "Grillmair Chimney" (5.5) on

Mount Laurie. C.S. was leading the fourth pitch when he pulled out a rock the size of a microwave. He fell approximately 5–7 meters with the rock and was caught by his belayer.

At 2145, some nearby campground staff reported a light shining midway up the mountain face. Twenty minutes later, C.H. arrived back to the parking lot and confirmed that his partner was in trouble on the mountain. He reported that C.S. had a broken wrist and was conscious.

Kananaskis Emergency Services personnel began to arrive on the scene and climb up the scree slopes to the base of the cliff. At 0100, two of the rangers began climbing the cliff towards the victim. As they were climbing in the dark, they did not arrive at the victim until 0615. They administered first aid to the victim's broken wrist and elbow, multiple contusions, cuts and abrasions. C.S. was then heli-slung out to the waiting ambulance. (Source: Kananaskis Country Alpine Specialist)

Analysis

Mount Laurie, better known as Yamnuska, is a popular limestone cliff on the eastern edge of the Canadian Rockies. The routes are up to 12 pitches in length, and most tend to be hard for their grade. The rock protection tends to be very good on the mountain, but the rock is also notoriously loose in sections, and it is not unusual for "microwave size blocks" to come undone. Every suspicious looking hand hold and foot hold must be tested completely before putting one's trust in it. (Source: Nancy Hansen)

FALL ON ICE, INADEQUATE PROTECTION, POOR POSITION, INEXPERIENCE and AVALANCHE (TWO SEPARATE ACCIDENTS)
Alberta, Banff National Park, Cascade Waterfall

These two serious accidents are reported together because they happened on the same climb within minutes of each other on December 17. They were separate and distinct accidents in one respect, but both incidents overlap in terms of terrain and the roles of the various people present.

Cascade Waterfall is one of the most accessible multi-pitch Grade III climbs in Western Canada. It is situated within sight of Banff town site, and consists of several hundred meters of ice beginning with easy lower-angled terrain leading up to three steeper main pitches of climbing. It is not uncommon for there to be several teams of climbers on Cascade at once. Like the majority of ice climbs in the Canadian Rockies, Cascade Waterfall is exposed to avalanche risk.

About 1400 on December 17, nine climbers in four separate parties were all positioned at various points along the main upper climb. One party of climbers had reached the end of pitch one, which is moderate Grade III. They decided to turn around and rappel back to the start of the pitch. When 21-year-old M., a beginner ice climber, reached the end of his rappel, he detached from the rope and began to walk across the low-angle ice. He was aiming for the ledge of dry rock which several others were using to exit the climb onto scree slopes to the east. Witnesses on the ledge say he took one or two steps, lost his balance and fell. He had no tools at hand and accelerated rapidly. He tumbled approximately

100 meters down the low-angled ice and came to rest on a broad ledge part way up the low-angled approach ice. All but two of the other climbers present were immediately aware of the accident and several began to descend toward M. by rappelling from the upper pitches or by down-climbing the scree route.

Meanwhile, two other climbers had reached the top of the main cliff and had walked a further 70 meters to a final 12-meter curtain which they both climbed. They were unaware they had reached the access to an alternate descent in the forested slopes to the west of the climb, and prepared to rappel the gully. They tried to install an Abalokov anchor several times, but found the ice at the lip of the curtain unsatisfactory. After 20 minutes, they finally chose a tree on the slope beside the gully. T. (31), a German national who was living and working in Calgary, rappelled to the foot of the curtain and detached from the rope on the flat snow at the foot of this ice step.

When his partner was halfway down his rappel, an avalanche came over the lip of the ice. One quarter of the main basin 200 meters further up the mountain had released. The climber on rappel immediately swung to his right away from the main volume of the slide. T. had no protection where he stood. He was hit by the full force of the avalanche and swept down the gradually steepening slope and over the main waterfall. He fell approximately 250 meters, coming to rest only a few meters from the victim of the first accident.

The avalanche occurred 15 minutes after the first accident. It caught everyone below in various stages of descending. The flying debris contained a large amount of loose rock which rained on the parties below. Some climbers were hit, but miraculously no one else was swept off or killed by the rock and ice fall.

All of the survivors were able to walk off the climb. Several were badly bruised and had broken bones. One climber spent a week in hospital in Calgary due to concern about kidney damage. Both the men who had fallen undoubtedly died almost instantly.

Analysis

Accident #1: Many climbers solo up to the point where this fatal accident occurred. In other words, it is "easy" grade 2 or 3 terrain. The difference is that climbers have ice tools in their hands when walking up the rolling steps. Due to his inexperience, M. misjudged the risk if he slipped while unroped and without an ice tool in his hand. The ice ramp below him was polished and unforgiving. He slipped seconds after detaching from the rappel, before anyone could warn him of the danger.

Accident #2: The avalanche hazard was rated "considerable" at treeline on December 17. By definition, "natural avalanches are possible" with this rating. Moderate snowfalls and steady winds had been gradually increasing the risk over the previous week. At the same time, one of the effects of the wind had been to strip snow from exposed terrain, giving the mountains in the Banff area the characteristic appearance that climbers have come to call "bony" or bare. On December 17, the terrain above Cascade Waterfall did not "look" very threatening.

This accident illustrates the difficult choices that are presented when the avalanche danger is in the mid-range of the scale. The party involved in the avalanche accident had considered the risk and decided to go anyway but to try and finish the climb as fast as possible in order to minimize their exposure. By midday, very strong warm winds had begun. The survivor said that about the time the slide hit them, he and his partner were concerned by the winds and by the fact it was taking them so long to get set up to go down.

There were seven other climbers on Cascade when the slide occurred. They all must have made some kind of calculation of the risk of climbing there that day. But one has to wonder to what extent any of them were also influenced simply by the presence of so many others on the climb. (Source: Parks Canada Warden Service)

FALL ON SNOW, NO HELMET, CLIMBING ALONE
British Columbia, Kootenay National Park, Mount Stanley

On August 6 a climber was reported overdue from a solo attempt on the Kahl route, a popular snow and ice alpine climb. He had been dropped off at 0600 at the trailhead and had been expected back by evening. The Warden Service was contacted at 2030. It is relatively common for climbers to be overdue on this route and usually when parties get benighted, they return by midday the following day. However, since the climber was solo, a search was initiated at first light the following morning. The climber was located in a rock gully below a snow slope on the usual descent route. He had fallen about 200 meters down the snow slope and eventually got hung up halfway down the gully. He died of the injuries sustained during the fall, including serious head lacerations.

Analysis

It appears from the subsequent investigation that the climber tried to self-arrest once he lost his footing. He was wearing crampons and it is possible that snow balled up underneath them, causing them to lose their effectiveness. His skid tracks went over a rock outcrop on the snow slope and he likely lost control of his self-arrest attempt at that point. In addition, he was carrying a technical ice tool which is not well suited for self arrest. Although he fell a considerable distance, a helmet may have reduced his head injuries and perhaps a different outcome may have ensued. (Source: Parks Canada Warden Service)

AVALANCHE, INEXPERIENCE
British Columbia, Mount Robson Provincial Park, Mount Robson

K.G. and M.J. (both 19) were in a party of four climbers who were camped near the Dome, a feature near the base of the Kain Face on Mount Robson. They left their basecamp at 0600 on August 15 to climb the Kain Face while the other two climbers remained at the basecamp. Their friends last saw the party at approximately 2230 at the top of the Kain Face. A big storm moved in during the night of August 15, which deposited several centimeters of heavy wet snow on the face.

On August 16, the two remaining climbers at basecamp on the Dome returned to Berg Lake, and at 1430 they reported their friends overdue. Meanwhile, the climbers on Robson bivouacked just above the Kain Face with no food and no extra clothing.

On the morning of August 16, the Kain Face was still in whiteout conditions. K.G. and M.J. began descending the face at approximately 0630. They were off route, and were at the far northwest edge of the face. As they down-climbed simultaneously, they were caught in three loose snow avalanches, but were able to arrest their falls with their ice axes. At 1100 a fourth avalanche carried them down the face. The climbers estimate that they were 200 meters from the top of the face when the fourth avalanche occurred. They were found on top of the avalanche deposit approximately 250 meters down the face.

The weather was poor on Mount Robson when the initial report was received. Robson park rangers were able to conduct an aerial search of the Kain Face area later during the day and at 1600 they requested that Jasper wardens attend the accident site for a rescue. The initial report was that the overdue party had fallen down the Kain Face and that one of the party members was moving but the other was not.

Banff wardens were also requested to assist. When the rescue party arrived from Jasper, both victims were moving. M.J. was on the flat terrain below the bergschrund and was sitting waving his arms, and K.G. was 100 meters up slope above the bergschrund, prone, with face down, slowly moving one hand only. They were located below an icefall, with serac fall creating an additional hazard for the rescuers. Poor weather, continuous avalanches from the face, and the threat of darkness were also factors in the rescue.

Both victims were slung out to the staging area via helicopter, where K.G. was med-evaced to Jasper Townsite. Amongst their injuries were broken ribs, collapsed lungs, fractured vertebrae, head injuries and multiple abrasions and lacerations.

Analysis
Neither had enough experience in mountaineering to attempt this climb. This was the first climb for one and third for the other. They had no training in navigation, snowpack evaluation, etc., and had no experience to draw on to make sound decisions. (Source: Parks Canada Warden Service)

ILLNESS
British Columbia, Glacier National Park, Mount Uto
On August 28, five climbers were on their way up the Southwest Ridge of Mount Uto, a 5.1 rock climb. One of the climbers, S.L. (F 45), developed sudden acute and severe right lower abdominal pain. The party managed to get her to a ledge where D.B. (43), a registered nurse, examined her abdomen. S.L. was showing symptoms of appendicitis. A decision was made that one experienced member of the party would descend alone to obtain help. Three hours later, S.L. was heli-slung off the mountain. The remaining three climbers rappelled and down-climbed. (Source: D.B.)

Analysis

While no accident occurred in this instance, this is a situation that could happen to any climber at any time. The party had a first aid kit with painkillers, which were of great help to the victim. The only regret the remaining party had was in only having one headlamp. Much of their descent was made in the dark due to the long wait for the rescue, and the descent would have been much easier and quicker if each person had a headlamp. (Source: D.B., Nancy Hansen)

WEATHER
British Columbia, Comox, Mount Albert-Edward

Three climbers were reported overdue on September 17. They had been attempting a four- to five-day traverse which involved glacier travel in the Mount Albert-Edward area in the Comox region of Vancouver Island. After spending two extra days out due to very bad weather, the climbers were located safe and sound as they hiked out. The previous year, two members of the same team had been airlifted from the same traverse when one member injured himself. (Source: Scott Larson, Provincial Emergency Program)

Analysis

The three climbers had the experience to complete this traverse safely. They were well prepared and had planned the trip well—including telling someone where they were and when they were expected back. When a nasty, unexpected weather front came upon them, they did a smart thing by waiting it out. They had the provisions for extra days and whiteout navigation could have resulted in their getting lost or finding themselves in dangerous terrain. (Source: Nancy Hansen)

SLIP ON ROCK, UNROPED, NO HARD HAT
Ontario, Milton, Buffalo Crag

On Sunday, March 28 F.M. (26) was scouting out the cliff top at Buffalo Crag, apparently hoping to set up a top rope on a climb called "Rainy Day Women." He had on a harness but was not tethered to an anchor. About 1300 he was seen falling, trying first to clutch at rocks and cedars, then tumbling to the rough talus 80 feet below. He suffered terrible head and internal injuries and possible broken bones. He was not wearing a helmet. He remained conscious for about an hour while climbers obtained the help of the Milton Fire Department rescue team. An air evacuation was requested, but the climber died as he was being transferred to the helicopter near the Rattlesnake Point Gatehouse.

Analysis

Beyond the obvious reminders to tether in and wear a helmet, it should be noted that this accident occurred in early spring, when melt-water increases cliff top hazard. The clay and the fine-grained dolomitic limestone at Buffalo Crag are very slippery when damp. (Source: David Henderson)

FALL ON ROCK, NO HARD HAT, PROTECTION PULLED, INEXPERIENCE
Ontario, Milton, Kelso Crags

On Sunday, August 15 P.D. (36) of Tonawanda, New York, began leading a 5.3 one-pitch route. He placed only sparse protection. Part way up, he switched to a nearby 5.6 route. After running into difficulties, he decided to back off. He slipped while down-climbing, pulled out his top piece of protection and fell 15 meters. He was not wearing a helmet and suffered a skull fracture and broken facial bones. His partner lowered the unconscious and bleeding climber. The Milton Fire Department evacuated him to the local hospital, and he was eventually transferred to a hospital in his hometown. He has since fully recovered and plans to return to the crags (with a helmet). His partner, however, has quit climbing.

Analysis

According to companions, P.D. was not an experienced lead climber. He did not place sufficient protection in the easier section of the pitch to prevent a long fall. A helmet would likely have reduced the severity of his injuries. To his credit, however, when P.D. ran into difficulties he did down-climb rather than try to muscle his way to the top. This shortened the length of the fall when it did occur. (Source: David Henderson)

UNITED STATES

AVALANCHE
Alaska, Wrangell St. Elias National Park and Preserve, University Range

James Haberl (41) from Whistler, BC, Keith Reid, and Graeme Taylor were climbing in the University Range of Wrangell St. Elias National Park and Preserve. The climbers were dropped off by Ultima Thule Outfitters on April 25 at the 6,000-foot level of a glacier in the University Range. The area had received about one and a half feet of new snow.

On April 28 the climbers left their camp about 0630 and traveled a mile or so to a location where they intended to traverse ridges to gain elevation and summit an unnamed peak. Winds were calm, the temperature was 15° C, and there were clear and sunny skies.

The slope they were on was 20–30-degrees and they were unroped. Haberl was about 30 yards in front of Reid and Taylor at the time of a slab release, just beneath Haberl. Reid and Taylor were able to cling to the ridge and stay out of the slow moving release. The slab was about 30 yards wide at the release point and about a yard deep. The slab gathered speed and poured over a 550–750-yard drop. Haberl traveled with the slab and went out of sight.

Reid and Taylor down-climbed for about two hours and located gloves, a hat and discolored snow. Probing attempts at the location of the discolored snow located Haberl. He was under about a yard of snow. Haberl had sustained very extensive head injuries.

Reid and Taylor attempted ground to air communications without success. They activated an emergency locator beacon and waited for air rescue. Ultima Thule Outfitters investigated the ELT and was given State Trooper permission to remove the body from the mountain. (Source: from an Alaska State Trooper report)

FALL ON SNOW, UNABLE TO SELF ARREST, NO BELAY
Alaska, Mount McKinley, West Buttress

A three-person Spanish expedition named "McKinley 99" began their expedition on May 3 from the 7,200-foot basecamp on the Kahiltna Glacier. Expedition members included Luis Ibanez (leader), Francisco Mira (33), and Jose Sanchez (39). They established a high camp at the 17,200-foot level on May 13. The next day, the team left in clear but windy conditions in an attempt to reach the summit. They climbed into increasingly windy conditions and were finally forced to retreat due to high winds after reaching a high point of 20,100 feet on the summit ridge about 1800. The three climbers descended roped together with Luis Ibanez leading, Sanchez second, and Mira following third. They did not utilize any running belay. Around 2000 the group reached a short steep icy section at 18,350 feet. While descending this section (known as "the autobahn"), Mira lost his footing and fell. Unable to self arrest Mira ultimately pulled Sanchez and Ibanez off their feet and the group continued down the slope approximately 500 feet distance before coming to a stop slightly above

17

Denali Pass. Ibanez, falling the shortest distance due to his position on the rope team, had no injuries while Mira received facial, wrist, shoulder, and upper leg injuries and Sanchez suffered ankle and rib injuries. Despite these, the men were able to descend the remaining 1,100 feet to their established camp at 17,200 feet by 2200.

On May 14 at 1000, Ibanez contacted an NPS Ranger patrol camping in the same area. Ibanez reported that his group had an accident and "need(s) some help." After evaluating the injured climbers and contacting the Talkeetna Ranger Station an air evacuation was coordinated. At 1345 the injured climbers were loaded into the NPS LAMA Helicopter and transported to the 7,000-foot basecamp. At 1359 the injured climbers were transferred to an NPS contracted fixed wing aircraft and flown to the Talkeetna airport. They were transferred to Providence Life Guard aircraft and transported to Providence hospital for treatment. Luis Ibanez descended to the 14,200-foot camp with assistance of the NPS patrol and continued to basecamp with other climbers.

Jose Sanchez and Francisco Mira were treated and released from Providence hospital. Sanchez's injuries included two left fractured ribs and a sprained right ankle. Mira's injuries included facial lacerations, broken nose, fractured left wrist, bruised left shoulder, and left thigh puncture wounds.

Analysis

The 18,300-foot level on the West Buttress has a history of falling accidents. The short, icy section of forty-five-degree terrain continues to prove itself a hazard for fatigued climbers descending from a summit attempt. Climbers, especially guides, have frequently set a short fixed line over this area to prevent accidents. A running belay would also avoid falls in this area. Despite its nonthreatening appearance, this area, and others like it, should be crossed with caution as even small injuries such as sprained ankles can have enormous consequences in high mountains. (Source: Kevin Moore, Mountaineering Ranger)

FALL ON SNOW, AMS
Alaska, Mount McKinley, West Buttress

The Denali Ski "Challenge 1999" expedition from Italy included skier Mauro Rumez and photographer Franco Toso. Their plan was to climb Denali by the West Rib and have Toso photograph Rumez as he skied the route.

They flew in on May 10 and began ascending the Northeast Fork of the Kahiltna Glacier on May 12, arriving at the bottom of the West Rib on May 14. Over the course of three days they climbed to 16,200 feet on the West Rib, camping there on May 17. The next day, Rumez left Toso and attempted to go to the summit, but was turned back by high winds at the "Football Field" (19,500 feet). Toso did not attempt to summit because he had AMS and was not feeling well. The climbers spent their second night together at 16,200 feet on the West Rib.

On May 19 they started to descend, with Rumez skiing and Toso on foot. Rumez skied the remainder of the route and stopped at 10,000 feet to watch Toso descend on his own. At 14,900 feet, Toso was making his way down through a serac field when he lost his footing and fell off a serac. Toso continued to slide, and fell over another serac cliff before stopping in some soft snow. Toso was unable to self arrest during the 65-foot fall. Rumez witnessed the fall and skied out the Northeast Fork to the 8,000-foot camp on the West Buttress looking for help. He contacted other climbers there and asked for assistance. Meanwhile, the Team Hung Low expedition from Crested Butte also witnessed Toso's fall and climbed up to Toso from their camp located at the second ice dome. Team Hung Low dialed 911 on a cell phone and explained the situation to the operator. The message was relayed to the Talkeetna Ranger Station at 1858.

At 2315, the LAMA helicopter piloted by Jim Hood brought a screamer suit to the scene where the injured Toso waited. Team Hung Low, who had been caring for Toso, prepared him for the short haul. Toso was lifted from the scene and flown down to Basecamp at 7,000 feet, where he was further stabilized by Park Service staff and volunteers. Toso was transferred to a Life Flight transport in Talkeetna and then flown to Anchorage Regional Hospital where he was treated for contusions to his right chest wall and left leg.

Analysis

Toso was unanchored when he lost his footing and fell. He was quite fortunate to stop in soft snow and come away with only contusions. The fact that he was experiencing Acute Mountain Sickness most likely played a role in his accident. (Source: Kevin Moore, Mountaineering Ranger)

EXCEEDING ABILITIES – OFF ROUTE, INADEQUATE EQUIPMENT AND WATER, HYPOTHERMIA, FROSTBITE
Alaska, Mount McKinley

On May 3, the Densan party from Great Britain arrived at Kahiltna basecamp, 7,200 feet on the Kahiltna Glacier. The three members of this expedition were Steve Ball (42), Antony Hollingshead (33), and Nigel Vardy (29). The team spent an average amount of time working their way up the West Rib route on Mount McKinley, 17 days to a high camp at approximately 15,900 feet. Climbing expedition style, carrying gear high and sleeping low as they moved upwards, the team reported that they were feeling acclimatized for their summit attempt.

At 0800 on May 19, the trio began their summit bid from the 15,900-foot level of the West Rib. Progress was made through the rocks and up the left of the two prominent couloirs on that route.

At 1730, an independent climber, Jack Tackle, contacted the group at the 18,800-foot level. Tackle was on a day climb from the 14,200-foot camp for acclimatizing and had set his own turnaround time for 1800. Tackle spoke with the group for 30 minutes. He noted that they did not have overnight gear, the climbing order was Ball, Hollingshead, Vardy, and that Ball had lost a glove. Tackle stated that the group was moving slowly but they were continuing up and also that they were too far right in the couloir consequently climbing steeper terrain than necessary. Tackle reported that the weather was calm at their location but that it was obviously blowing hard off of the summit plateau. One and a half hours later Tackle was back at the 14,200-foot camp and noted through binoculars that the Densan party had only progressed a few rope lengths. At that time the weather had deteriorated to the point that there was a visible lenticular over the summit. Tackle expressed his concerns about the party to ranger Kevin Moore that evening.

At 2200, the Densan team arrived on the summit plateau at 19,600 feet. Discovering that their water bottles had frozen, they were unable to hydrate themselves because of not bringing along a stove and pot. The clouds were obscuring their visibility so they proceeded on a compass bearing toward the summit. As they continued higher, the south summit would disappear in and out of the clouds.

Just after midnight on May 20, exhausted, they decided to rest in a small crevasse that they estimated to be 300–400 feet below the summit on the southeast side. According to Hollingshead, Vardy's eye was swollen shut due to current frostbite on an area that had previously been sunburned. Ball was shivering from hypothermia most of the time they attempted to rest, and no one was able to sleep.

At 0300, the team radioed a "Mayday" that was received by Tim Stageberg at the Kahiltna basecamp. Stageberg notified National Park Service Ranger Meg Perdue, and she was able to determine that the British party was requesting a rescue because one of their members was injured and unable to descend. Perdue's communications consisted of a series of yes or no questions that the Densan party would respond to with either one or two clicks of their radio because their battery power was too weak to transmit voice.

The Densan party began descending about 0430. At one point Vardy fell and pulled the others down the slope a short distance. The three were able to traverse the Football Field with considerable time and effort back to the top of the "Orient Express" (19,500 feet on West Rib) where they had ascended. The team debated rappelling the route and lowering Vardy back to their high camp, but chose instead to descend the less technically difficult West Buttress route. As they began to descend it became apparent that Vardy was unable to continue because he could not walk more than a few feet without falling down. So at 1330 it was decided that Ball, being the strongest, would descend the West Buttress alone in order to summon help.

Incident Commander JD Swed received a call from Perdue at his residence at 0400. National Park Service staff were summoned and the Rescue Coordination Center (RCC) was alerted. At 0830, an LC 130 launched from Anchorage and upon arrival over Mount McKinley, began passing weather observations to the ICP and receiving transmissions from the injured party on CB channel 19. These transmissions were only squelch breaks with no voice.

At 1122 Jay Hudson launched from Talkeetna in his Cessna 206 with ranger George Beilstein on board. They were able to make a pass at the 19,300-foot level and Beilstein saw three people—two standing and one lying down. Because of turbulence, Hudson descended and landed at basecamp. The National

Park Service high altitude LAMA helicopter was also positioned at Kahiltna basecamp and made three different attempts throughout the afternoon to get to the Densan Party. Meanwhile a ground rescue team of five climbers was ascending from the 14,200-foot camp.

The LAMA piloted by Jim Hood was able to deliver a pack of survival gear to two rescuers at the 16,700-foot level on the West Rib. On the fifth attempt the LAMA was able to deliver a pack to the Densan party at 2219 (this Dana Design backpack containing a Park Service radio, CB radio, thermos, MSR Wisperlite stove, North Face Tangerine Dream sleeping bag, ridge rest ensolite pad, and food was subsequently abandoned.)

Voice radio contact was established with the British climbers at 2250 via the new radios in the pack. It was determined that Vardy was the most critical patient, with frostbitten face and hands and a severe loss of coordination. Hollingshead reported that he also had frostbite on his hands and that he had bruised his right shoulder in the fall. The NPS also learned at this time that Ball had separated from the party at 1330 and was planning to descend the West Buttress. Based on the reconnaissance that Hood preformed while delivering the pack at 19,500 feet, it was decided to short haul the two patients off using a screamer suit. It was determined after Lead Climbing Ranger Daryl Miller talked with both climbers on the park radio that Miller would instruct Hollingshead on the procedures of short hauling. Hollingshead placed the screamer suit on Vardy then hooked him into the "God Ring," hanging from the 100-foot rope hooked to the NPS LAMA. Vardy was safely on the glacier at basecamp at 2323 following his five minute short haul ride down from 19,500 feet. Hollingshead was picked up in the same manner just after midnight and landed at basecamp. Vardy and Hollingshead were then flown by Hudson to Talkeetna where the lifeguard air ambulance took them to Providence Medical Center in Anchorage.

A brief interview with the two British climbers in Talkeetna provided rangers with information on Steve Ball. Ball intended to descend the West Buttress route as far as need be to get help for his team. He had a few snacks, a map and compass, but no water. On the evening of May 20 there were no climbers camped at the 17,200-foot level. On the morning of the May 21 several private parties departed 14,200 for high camp and ranger Kevin Moore alerted them to look for Ball who was wearing a red insulated parka over orange and black wind stopper fleece. At 1056 a Cessna 310 was launched from Talkeetna with Ranger Joe Reichert on board to make an air search of the routes that Ball could have descended. The plane was on scene over the summit plateau by 1120 and made over 20 passes in a linear pattern without spotting Ball. At 1112 a Cessna 185 chartered from Hudson's Air Service and piloted by Don Bowers departed Talkeetna to continue the aerial search at lower elevations. Due to deteriorating weather, the 310 returned to Talkeetna at 1300. About this time a ground team reported that they had spotted Ball below Denali Pass. Within ten minutes Paul Berry, Dave Lucy, Stuart Parks, Thomas Ryan, and Richard Cariter had arrived on scene and reported to NPS via CB radio that the person was indeed Ball and that he was conscious but severely hypothermic and had an open fracture of the left tibia and fibula. Parks reported that there was a possible landing zone for the helicopter 40 feet up slope from Ball. At 1351 the LAMA was en route directly to 17,200 feet. At 1407 the ground team received directions to administer a dose of Decadron via injection. Pilot Jim Hood inspected the site at 1450 and determined that there was too much of a slope for a landing, so he passed off a supply of batteries and descended to basecamp to receive a new plan. Over the following two hours the weather was unsettled. The ground team began lowering Ball toward the camp at 17,200 feet. At 1600 the LAMA launched from basecamp with the Bauman bag and a backboard connected to the end of the short haul rope. At 1620 the cargo was delivered to the rescuers at 17,700 feet and the LAMA returned to basecamp. Based on the power checks that Hood made when delivering the Bauman bag it was determined that a short haul would be performed to extract Ball before the weather deteriorated further. At 1645 the LAMA lifted off of basecamp with ranger Billy Shott attached to the short haul rope and ascended to 17,700 feet. On scene Shott attached the Bauman Bag to the short haul rope in a tandem configuration and returned to basecamp at 1717. An Air National Guard Pavehawk transported Ball to Providence Medical Center.

Analysis

This unfortunate accident was a classic example of a party overextending themselves and being caught by the temperamental weather on Mount McKinley. Had they set a turnaround time and adhered to it, the rescue may have been avoided. A stove may have allowed them to rehydrate and revitalize their energy once the situation had become serious. All members carried frozen water bottles; hence, they were unable to utilize their water. Also, because of the dehydration, altitude sickness, and exposure to the high wind this team became dysfunctional, precluding any safe descent. They were forced to bivi at 19,500 feet, which was one of many questionable decisions made regarding their safety. Another note is the unfortunate trend among outdoor enthusiasts to rely more heavily on their technological means of communication to call for help in the event of emergency than to be prepared for such an event and remain self sufficient. The combination of dehydration, fatigue, and cold were nearly lethal for this team. (Source: Joe Reichert, Mountaineering Ranger)

(Editor's Note: Jack Tackle's observation of the ascent indicated that the party was certainly not acclimatized to do a summit bid starting from 15,400 feet. Their ascent rate was about 250 feet per hour, by his calculations.)

FALLING ICE, FALL ON ICE, ICE SCREW FAILED
Alaska, Thunder Mountain

On May 12 Malcolm Daly (43) and Jim Donini (57) of Boulder, Colorado flew onto the Tokositna Glacier at 7,500 feet to attempt a new route on Mount Hunter (14,573 feet). The Colorado team spotted a potential route on Thunder Mountain (10,970 feet)—a satellite of Mount Hunter—which has a short approach from the airstrip. Daly and Donini started climbing a couloir containing mixed ice, snow, and rock, with a technical difficulty that included some Grade 6 ice steps. The Colorado team spent the next several days climbing up the couloir and returning to their basecamp each night. During the next several days Daly and Donini experienced several problems on the Thunder Mountain route. Donini had crampon points fail, and Daly was hit with a chunk of ice or rock that numbed his arm requiring them to return to basecamp.

On May 21st at 0300, Daly and Donini continued their climb in the couloir reaching the high point at approximately 2,500 feet above the glacier. At 1030, Daly, who was leading the pitch believes he was hit with a chunk of snow or ice that knocked him off the route. Donini was able to hold the fall even though he was struck by Daly's crampons. Daly was knocked unconscious, but regained consciousness shortly thereafter and was able to talk to Donini. The one piece of protection that failed during the fall was a short ice screw 15 feet below Daly. Daly had put several ice screws on a vertical pillar 70 feet below and then climbed a lower-angle snow ramp to the vertical section on which he fell. After the fall Donini rigged an ice ax as a splint and wrapped tape around Daly's boots in an effort to stabilize both his legs. Donini lowered Daly approximately 200 feet, but then decided that without air splints or some other means of stabilizing Daly's open fractures he might bleed to death or go into shock. They both decided the best choice was for Donini to descend to get help. Donini was able to rappel some of the route and down-climbed the lower section. Paul Roderick of Talkeetna Air Taxi who was flying over the site at the time spotted Donini and landed. Donini and Roderick departed the Tokositna Glacier at 1800 and flew to Talkeetna. During the flight Roderick called via his cell phone and reported the incident to the Ranger Station. Donini was treated at the Ranger Station and later was driven to the Sunshine Clinic and treated for his puncture wound.

At 1947, South District staff were notified of the incident and asked to return to the Ranger Station. The Chief Ranger, RCC, Air National Guard, Hudson Air Service, and the NPS LAMA were also called and briefed of the incident. The NPS LAMA helicopter attempted to fly with mountaineering rangers Billy Shott, George Beilstein, and Daryl Miller to Thunder Mountain incident site. Minutes before lift off, Talkeetna Air Taxi owner Paul Roderick arrived at the NPS Helicopter pad advising the LAMA pilot Karl Cotton that the weather had shut down in the range.

On May 22 at 0820, the NPS LAMA lifted off with mountaineering rangers Miller, Shott, and Beilstein aboard en route to the Thunder Mountain accident site. The Rescue Coordination Center launched an Air National Guard Pavehawk helicopter with three PJs aboard and a C 130 for weather and communication support. The Denali South District Incident Command Center also used a Cessna 206 from Hudson Air Service for a weather observation aircraft.

The LAMA landed at 0905 on the Tokositna Glacier at the base of Thunder Mountain. Rescue gear was unloaded and the LAMA flew to the accident site and attempted a power check above Daly. The clouds moved in and out, obscuring the view around the site and cliffs above. After several minutes, LAMA pilot Jim Hood stated that a short haul would not be possible due to the present weather conditions, as well as the possibility of falling debris and the extreme danger of the LAMA's rotors being too close to the mountain. Another site approximately 1,000 feet above Daly was considered for a lowering/raising possibility. The snow dome was not large enough to safely land the LAMA, but the site did offer short haul possibilities. The dome appeared sufficient in size to short haul two persons at a time and large enough for eight rescuers total to work. The team would bring rescue gear, ropes, and bivy gear, along with food for four to five days in case inclement weather prevented the LAMA from flying.

At 0950, the Air National Guard Pavehawk landed at the Tokositna Glacier site with three PJs. The PJs unloaded medical supplies and rescue gear and set up a basecamp including a large tent that could be used to treat Daly's injuries. Clouds had obscured the accident site, and only part of Thunder Mountain was visible. Daryl Miller and LAMA pilot Karl Cotton departed the Tokositna Glacier for Talkeetna at 1100. Present weather conditions prevented any SAR activities requiring aviation support at the accident site. Miller debriefed Donini regarding the accident including route conditions and Daly's mental/physical condition. Donini stated that Daly was in a "positive" mental state when he left him. Donini stated that he felt both ankles were broken with some bleeding occurring and had cut the boot strings because of the feet swelling. Donini had given Daly extra clothing layers and left him with some food and water. Donini reported that the route was extremely technical in places and had objective hazards with potential rock/ice coming down the couloir at different times. He also had used some of the fixed line left in place to rappel the more technical sections.

Miller and Cotton departed in the LAMA to the Thunder Mountain accident site at 1700 to attempt a site evaluation and power check for the lowering from the dome 1,000 feet above Daly. The weather was extremely cloudy and forced the LAMA to land at the 7,200-foot Kahiltna basecamp. After repeated attempts to fly to the accident site, the LAMA returned to Talkeetna.

On May 23 at 0750, Miller and Cotton flew from Talkeetna to the Thunder Mountain accident site. Weather was clear and stable in the range. En route, Miller and Cotton discussed the possibility of short hauling Daly using a longer rope, doubling the distance to 200 feet. One of the key problems on May 22 in addition to the weather was the 400–500-foot V-shaped cliff side of the couloir, which impaired rotor clearance for the LAMA. The plan was to lower a Ranger below Daly on the snow ramp, then climb to Daly and clip him into the "God Ring." The LAMA had 30 feet or more of rotor clearance from the cliff sides and good light conditions. Cotton felt he could do the mission if he had a spotter aboard to watch for rotor clearance and also to observe the short hauler.

At 0810 the LAMA landed and Cotton talked via radio with the incident command center in Talkeetna to get an OK for the short haul. After the permission was granted, a 100-foot doubled section of short haul rope was cut and tied into the main line. Ranger Billy Shott was selected for the short haul position and Ranger Meg Perdue was selected as the observer inside the LAMA. Cotton, Shott, Perdue, and Miller discussed the mission and agreed that Shott would not unclip at the accident site.

The LAMA lifted off the glacier with Meg Perdue and Shott at the end of the short haul rope. Perdue's mission was to watch Shott, give Cotton information on the area weather and distances from the right cliff sides. On the first attempt to place Shott on the snowfield below Daly, a cloud moved in and Cotton aborted the mission. The cloud moved through the couloir and the LAMA repositioned placing Shott 75 feet below Daly on the 50–60-degree snowfield. Shott lost all radio communication after he landed on the snowfield and had to rely on hand signals. Shott used the LAMA for a belay and climbed to Daly in several minutes. Shott clipped Daly's harness into the "God Ring" with daisy chain and locking carabiner. Shott also put a chest harness on Daly and checked to make sure all the anchors were cut. Shott then gave the LAMA a hand signal indicating they were ready to lift off.

At 0927 the LAMA landed Daly at the LZ on the glacier airstrip, and personnel lowered him into a stretcher. Daly was immediately transferred into a medical tent where his fractures were splinted and a secondary survey completed. A Life Flight helicopter landed at the site, and Daly was loaded and transported to Providence Hospital in Anchorage.

Analysis

This was a complicated high-risk rescue that involved a multi-agency team which became a high profile event with the media. Daly and Donini were extremely experienced and competent mountaineers who had planned Mount Hunter as their primary climb and Mount Thunder as a pre-climb. Donini had previously climbed many Alaskan alpine technical routes. Between the two of them there was a wealth of mountaineering knowledge. They both were physically fit allowing them to climb fast on alpine routes, which demanded minimal time on certain sections.

They were also extremely cautious in climbing this particular route at the right time of day, which generally was during the cold. Daly believes that prior to his fall he was in a solid stance, but remembers the integrity of the ice was questionable but nothing else regarding the event that caused the fall. With only one piece (ice screw) 15 below him, questionable ice, and no protection for the next 70 feet, he was at high risk if he fell. An additional piece of protection may have reduced the severity of the fall. Daly estimated initially he fell about 140 feet, but after they looked at pictures, they concluded it was approximately 200 feet. Donini's remarkable descent for help and the timing of Paul Roderick flying over were key elements in Daly surviving this event. The rescue scenarios without short hauling were extremely complicated and risky to the rescuers and Daly. After the initial assessment of pilot Jim Hood regarding a "no go" for the short haul, the rescue team looked at other strategies. The first option was to lower an attendant and litter from an ice/snow dome 1,000 feet above Daly and then reverse the system and raise both Daly and the attendant back up. Raising Daly seemed safer than lowering the 2,500 feet to the glacier floor, which would have exposed Daly and the attendant to possible falling rock and ice. Also, the two ropes would have run the risk of being cut because of the many edge protection devices required to cover the numerous steps down the couloir. Other options discussed were to climb from the bottom, fixing the couloir up to Daly and lowering Daly back down the couloir. This rescue scenario seemed feasible at first because it was not dependent on aircraft or weather conditions. The dilemma was the 2,500-foot couloir had many objective hazards that would have put the rescuers at an unjustified risk for a substantial period of time. The last option was climbing to the top of Thunder Mountain via a ridge system and lowering an attendant to Daly and attempt to raise both persons back to the top. All these options were discussed and evaluated regarding risk assessment and saving Daly's life.

Without the remarkable flying ability, spotter assistance inside the helicopter, and a courageous short hauler, Daly's chances were dismal. All the rescue personnel, including the incident command system in Talkeetna and medical staff on scene, were key elements contributing to Daly's surviving this accident. Daly's positive attitude and will to live contributed to his survival.

One final note: Several hours after this remarkable short haul rescue, the weather in the Alaska range shut down for almost one week. (Source: Daryl R. Miller, Mountaineering Ranger)

FATIGUE, DEHYDRATION, FROSTBITE, CLIMBING ALONE
Alaska, Mount McKinley, West Buttress

Tomoyasu Ishikawa (30) began his solo ascent of Mount McKinley from the Kahiltna Glacier on May 19. He arrived at the 14,200-foot camp on the 21st where he planned to climb the Messner Couloir. On May 24 at 1100, he started his ascent of the couloir. He reached the top of the couloir at 1500 where he encountered strong winds and whiteout conditions. From the top of the couloir at 19,200 feet, Ishikawa decided to bivouac. With no stove or sleeping bag, he wrapped himself in a tarp, using hand warmers for supplemental heat. He remained at this site until 1330 on the 25th, and then he continued toward the summit.

At 1600 Ishikawa was attempting to photograph on the summit ridge when he noticed that he had frostbitten fingers. The frostbite caused him alarm, so he decided to descend the West Buttress. At 1900 he reached the 17,200-foot camp. At 1915 Toby Grohne of the "Alley Cats" party radioed to the 14,200-foot Ranger Station that they were providing aid to Ishikawa. Ranger Roger Robinson of the 14,200-foot camp had Grohne search out a mountain guide in the 17,200-foot camp. At 1935, guide Weslie Bunch of Mountain Trip Guide Service reported that Ishikawa was exhausted with frostbitten fingers and nose but would not need a rescue. Robinson advised Bunch of the emergency gear in the cache including tent, sleeping bag, and pads. At 2004 Bunch informed Robinson that they had placed Ishikawa with Mike and Norm Johnson of "AK

UT Mountain Sickness" expedition. The Johnsons began hydrating Ishikawa, as his only fluid consumption had been one liter that he drank on the 24th. By the morning on the 26th, Ishikawa felt stronger. At 1300 the Johnsons reported that Ishikawa would be descending with the five-member "Korean 99" party to 16,200 feet. Robinson arranged for his patrol to assist Ishikawa down the fixed lines. At 1434 patrol members DJ Nechrony and Rod Willard met Ishikawa on the fixed lines and began lowering him. Robinson, VIP Joel Geisendorfer, and PJ John Loomis, along with Nechrony and Willard, assisted Ishikawa back to the 14,200-foot camp, arriving at 1645 .

VIP Dr. Bob Desiderio and Willard treated Ishikawa. He had frostbite on the middle three fingers of his right hand and the last three fingers of his left hand. He also suffered frostbite on his nose with minor cold injuries to his toes. Robinson felt that Ishikawa should be evacuated from the 14,200-foot camp due to the limited use of his hands and the fact that he was solo climbing.

Poor weather prevented his evacuation until the 31st. At 1005 the LAMA helicopter was able to land at 14,200 feet. Ishikawa was flown to the Kahiltna basecamp where he was transferred to a Talkeetna Air Taxi fixed wing aircraft and flown out to Talkeetna and transported by a shuttle service to Providence Hospital where he was admitted in the evening of the 31st.

Analysis

Here is a good example of a solo climber relying on the assistance of others. Without this help, Tomoyasu Ishikawa may well have suffered further injury. A solo climber in trouble will add to the burden of private climbers and rescuers where the situation may only be an inconvenience when climbers are climbing in a group. (Source: Roger Robinson, Mountaineering Ranger)

INADEQUATE FOOD AND WATER, CLIMBING ALONE
Alaska, Mount McKinley, West Buttress

Shigeo Tamoi (33) began his solo climb of Mount McKinley's West Buttress on May 28. He ascended to the 14,200-foot camp in three days and then he acclimatized for three more days. On June 3 at 0700 Tamoi attempted a one-day ascent from the 14,200-foot camp carrying no survival gear, minimum clothing, and one liter of water. He was reported to have reached the summit in the evening and then descended to the 19,500-foot level (Football Field) where he collapsed on the trail. The temperature was approximately 25°F and the wind was 10 mph. Michal Krissak of the "Slovak Expedition 99" was also soloing down from the summit when he noticed a group of five climbers standing around Tamoi. As he approached on the trail, the five climbers left Tamoi behind and continued their descent. Krissak encountered Tamoi at 2100 lying face down, semi-conscious. Initially Krissak was unable to arouse Tamoi, but eventually Tamoi said he was thirsty and wanted to sleep. Krissak knew the situation for Tamoi was life threatening in the bitter cold if he didn't try to get him down. Krissak was able to lift Tamoi to his feet and support him under his shoulder. They had walked a short distance when three other descending climbers approached them. The three were unwilling to assist Krissak. He argued with them to at least give Tamoi some water or he might die. They finally gave Tamoi a little to drink then continued their descent leaving Krissak to deal with Tamoi.

The descent went very slowly with Krissak supporting Tamoi. Upon reaching Denali Pass, three American climbers approached the pair on their descent. By this time Krissak was tired and knew he needed Tamoi on a belay in order to safely descend the traverse. Krissak told the Americans about Tamoi's condition and asked if they could put him on their rope. The Americans refused to help and stated that they were cold and needed to keep going down. Krissak was again left to deal with Tamoi. Without a rope, Krissak began the traverse from the pass by supporting Tamoi from the rear. Tamoi could barely support his own weight. Twice he lost his footing and was held in place by Krissak.

At 0100 Tamoi and Krissak arrived exhausted to the 17,200-foot camp. Krissak began calling for help on his CB radio when NPS VIP Joel Geisendorfer and Alaska Air National Guardsman John Loomis who were camped nearby offered their assistance. Tamoi was provided fluids and a sleeping bag. While Tamoi slept in the supine position, Geisendorfer heard him vomit. He was able to clear Tamoi's airway. The pair began hydrating Tamoi first thing in the morning. At 1000 Tomai was able to descend to the 14,200-foot camp with a Korean party. Tomai was able to continue descending without assistance to the landing strip where he flew off on June 5th.

Analysis

Shigeo Tamoi is a pretty lucky man. Without the persistent efforts of Michal Krissak, Tamoi would certainly have been left for dead. Krissak risked his own life where others refused under the harsh conditions. It is hard to blame these other climbers, as sometimes it's just about impossible to help someone if you feel your own life at risk. This ranger heard about Tamoi's rescue from the staff at the 17,000-foot camp and had to literally search out Krissak in order to document this remarkable incident. Even then Krissak felt he did nothing out of the ordinary. When Ranger Daryl Miller interviewed Tamoi through an interpreter in Talkeetna, he found that Tamoi couldn't remember his summit day, the rescue, or even returning to the 14,200-foot camp. (Source: Roger Robinson, Mountaineering Ranger)

INEXPERIENCE, FAILURE TO TURN BACK
Alaska, Mount McKinley, West Buttress

Mike McCarthy (32) faxed his Mount McKinley climbing registration form to the Talkeetna Ranger Station on March 16. His climbing experience consisted of three hikes up Long's Peak in Rocky Mountain National Park. Ranger George Beilstein reviewed the registration form then called McCarthy on March 19. Beilstein was concerned about McCarthy's lack of experience and emphasized his concerns about solo glacier travel. McCarthy stated that he was aware of the hazards and would try to find a partner. No other contact was made until May 16, when McCarthy checked in for his climb at the Talkeetna Ranger

Station. Ranger Daryl Miller gave McCarthy his McKinley briefing and also advised him that as "he had no mountaineering or glacier experience, he was extremely foolish to solo on the glacier without a climbing partner." He advised McCarthy that "his life was in extreme danger" if he attempted to climb solo and that possibly he would endanger other lives as well.

McCarthy opted to go against Miller's advice and climb solo up the West Buttress route starting on May 17. McCarthy carried only an 8-foot 2"x2" piece of wood for crevasse protection. A 2"x2" spanning seven feet would support approximately 100 pounds at its midpoint. McCarthy weighed 230 pounds. Combining the weight of his pack and sled, the total weight was closer to 330 pounds. McCarthy was observed carrying the 2"x2" in his hands at right angles to his direction of travel. Even if it held him, it would have proved ineffectual since it was carried parallel to the crevasses.

A climbing party reported that McCarthy was assisted putting on his tent fly. It appears he couldn't figure out how to do this. Another climbing party witnessed McCarthy step one leg into a crevasse near the 7,800-foot camp. On the 26th, McCarthy arrived at the 14,200-foot camp with the assistance of Witek Szalankiewicz, another solo climber. Szalankiewicz took pity on McCarthy at 11,000 feet where McCarthy was already running low on fuel and high energy food. McCarthy's stove was set up with a diesel burning jet which consumes white gas twice as fast as he had planned. On May 28, Szalankiewicz reported to Ranger Roger Robinson that he was concerned about McCarthy's health and his ability to descend without assistance. He explained to Robinson that McCarthy had no energy possibly due to AMS and a poor diet. He also stated that McCarthy had no climbing experience, which was evident when McCarthy displayed difficulty descending below 14,200 feet to retrieve a cache. He explained that McCarthy had to step sideways to get down a very low-angle slope. He also mentioned that McCarthy had lost one of his mittens near Windy Corner and didn't have a spare. On May 29, Szalankiewicz convinced McCarthy to go over to the Ranger Station and have his SPO2 checked. His SPO2 (oxygen saturation level) registered in the mid 80s, indicating he was likely acclimating well to the 14,000-foot level. Szalankiewicz indicated that he would continue soloing and leave McCarthy and that he would possibly descend at some point. Several private climbers and members in Robinson's patrol tried to talk McCarthy into descending, but to no avail.

Many climbers on the mountain shared their concerns with Robinson. On June 1 Kellie Kenny of the "Alaskan Kennymore Krew" party reported to Robinson that she had heard him state, "It is going to be either this [Denali] or Kevorkian—but Kevorkian is in jail." On June 2 Simon Pageot and Kathleen Michaud of the "Friends on Denali" party reported that McCarthy told them that he had lost his job in Chicago and decided to take all his stuff to Alaska to live. It was Pageot's opinion that McCarthy was going through a depression.

Robinson was concerned about McCarthy's mental stability and his complete lack of climbing experience. Robinson felt that McCarthy could crawl higher but didn't have the expertise to climb back down. Robinson hoped that

McCarthy would join some group going down and descend with them.

On June 3, Robinson and VIP Dr. Bob Desiderio were descending the fixed lines. At 2000 they encountered McCarthy at the base of the lines at 15,500 feet. Robinson informed McCarthy that he "had accomplished a lot to have gotten this far and no one would have expected you to have reached this height. It's now time to head back down." He didn't appear to take Robinson seriously, so Robinson continued: "Over the years I have seen four other solo climbers with similar experience of which three died and the fourth was rescued. I don't want you to end up getting injured or worse…dead." Robinson made one final warning: "If you continue up and cause any problems, your climb will be finished and we will bring you down." After this McCarthy didn't say much, but he thanked Robinson for the advice. Robinson offered McCarthy a spot on his rope so he could safely descend back to the 14,200-foot camp, but McCarthy declined. Later that evening several climbers reported seeing McCarthy ascending the fixed lines on his hands and knees, not attached to his ascender, but instead using it as a hand hold.

Sean Sullivan, chief guide of an Alpine Ascents International party, provided the following statement: "On 4 June, I spoke with Michael McCarthy at 16,200 feet. He was cooking in the open and said he was very low on energy; he had no desire to go up or down and wasn't sure what to do. I encouraged him to descend, but he said he felt it would be a waste of his time. I told him that his listlessness was probably a sign of AMS and he thought it wasn't a big deal. Later I spoke to him again about 200 feet higher as he was on his way up. I asked if he was sure he should go up, and he said he couldn't think of any reason not to. When I said that I could think of lots of reasons, he said, 'Yeah, I guess I can too, but oh, well.' He continued on toward 17,200 feet."

At 1850 on the 4th, Dr. Dan Hansen of the "Eagle River Denali" party noticed McCarthy at the base of Washburn's Thumb wearing no gloves and appearing very lethargic. He observed that his fingers had the appearance of "sausage digits"—all swollen with cuts. McCarthy arrived late in the evening of the 4th to the 17,200-foot camp where he set up camp. In the afternoon of the 5th, VIP Joel Geisendorfer was surprised to find McCarthy getting ready to go to the summit. Geisendorfer tried to talk him out of going up, especially so late in the day. Geisendorfer discovered that McCarthy hadn't planned to take any survival gear, so he encouraged him to take his sleeping bag, stove, climbing harness and snow saw. McCarthy departed at 1430, ascending mostly on his hands and knees straight up next to the rocks. This steep, seldom used route proved very slow going for McCarthy. At 2300 he had climbed 1500 feet to the 18,700-foot level. McCarthy chopped a small ledge on the 45-degree icy slope and went to sleep in his bag. He did not anchor himself in on the open slope. This night proved to be a very calm with no wind and the minimum temperature at -20° F at the 17,200-foot level. Previously the upper mountain had been plagued for weeks with very cold temperatures and strong winds. McCarthy was extremely fortunate for this weather break in his exposed, open bivouac. He didn't move until 1400 on the 6th, at which time he traversed the slope down toward Denali Pass. From here McCarthy descended from the pass very slowly on the established traverse route back to 17,200 feet. McCarthy was near the bottom of the traverse at 17,500 feet, but still above the rock band where he slipped and began to cartwheel down the slope at 1730. He tumbled approximately 100 feet over the rocks and over a large bergschrund, stopping himself with his crampons. He was very lucky to have stopped and to have sustained only minor bruises. Alaska Air National Guardsman, John Loomis, and solo climber Artur Testov traversed over to McCarthy and assisted him back to the 17,200-foot camp. They informed Robinson of the situation. Robinson informed McCarthy by radio that he "was through with his climb and that we would be assisting him down." McCarthy accepted Robinson's declaration.

McCarthy had consumed just a half liter of fluid since leaving the high camp, so the plan was made to get McCarthy hydrated and assist his descent the next day if weather was good. On June 7 at 1130 Geisendorfer, Testov, and Loomis began their descent by belaying McCarthy down the ridge. Loomis noted that McCarthy didn't know how to properly put on his climbing harness or open a locking carabiner. Since McCarthy had difficulty descending, Testov short roped him while on belay. At 1230 Robinson, VIP DJ Nechrony, and VIP Rod Willard joined the descending party at 17,000 feet and began fixing a 600-foot rope down the ridge. The fixed line was leapfrogged down the ridge while Testov continued with McCarthy on belay. The 16,200-foot fixed lines were reached at 1700. McCarthy was put on a separate belay using the 600-foot rope. They reached the 14,200-foot camp at 1900. Since McCarthy was a tremendous liability to himself and others, Robinson felt he should be escorted all the way down to basecamp. Time was near for Robinson's patrol to descend so Geisendorfer and Alaska Air National Guardsman Lynn Graybill volunteered to take McCarthy down. At 2000 on the 8th, the three departed, arriving at the 7,200-foot basecamp at 0800 on the 9th. McCarthy was flown off the mountain later that day by Talkeetna Air Taxi.

Analysis

Here is an example of someone who should never have been allowed to climb Mount McKinley. Mike McCarthy had read a book about Reinhold Messner and the book *Into Thin Air* and felt he wanted to do something like that. With absolutely no climbing experience, he set off to do a near suicide mission. He never figured that others might be at risk if he failed. Every attempt was made by the Park Service and numerous other climbers to get him to turn around even though we felt obligated to provide assistance. This same assistance enabled him to go higher. If he had continued to the upper reaches of the mountain, there is no doubt in my mind that he would have been a fatality. While McCarthy was on the mountain, every day I was asked by climbers, "Why do you let him go up?" and "Why can't you do something about him?" These climbers had put in years of preparation to climb here and then to witness this debacle unfold! These climbers also knew that they might get stuck with trying to save this guy's life. It is this ranger's opinion that future Mike McCarthy's should be screened and denied permission to climb. This situation was an embarrassment to our education program and our credibility among climbers and the general public. (Source: Roger Robinson, Mountaineering Ranger) *(Editor's Note: It seems as though McCarthy must also have read* Into the Wild... *Several years ago, a young man wrote to this park and asked, "Is there snow on Mount McKinley all year round and will I have to make camps along the way?" The National Park Service has the same remedy as the U.S. Coast Guard for individuals who put themselves and others at risk. A citation for "Creating a Hazard" may be issued and may include a fine.)*

SNOW BLINDNESS, ACUTE MOUNTAIN SICKNESS
Alaska, Mount McKinley
On June 15, both a South African McKinley expedition, consisting of Ian Bailey, Steve Camp, and Anthony Tonder, and a Taiwan Chen expedition consisting of Boa Hwan You and Mei Hsing Chen, returned to the 17,200-foot camp after reaching Mount McKinley's summit. The South African expedition had taken twelve days to summit and the Chen expedition had taken ten days. Both expeditions had experienced difficulty on their summit days and received assistance from another expedition while descending. Ian Bailey had began to suffer the effects of snow blindness while descending from the summit and Boa Hwan You contemplated a forced bivouac while descending due to exhaustion and severe acute mountain sickness (possibly high altitude pulmonary edema). On June 16 at the 17,200-foot camp around 0900, contact was made with the two groups. Both Bailey and You were evaluated and treated by an NPS Ranger for snow blindness and AMS.

At 0110 the South African and Chen expeditions began descending from 17,200 feet to 14,200 feet with an NPS Ranger organizing the descent. Short rope, running belay, and lowering techniques were used to safely reach the 14,200-foot camp. Once in camp Bailey was treated for snow blindness by NPS personnel, given medical supplies, and released. Bailey, with his other two expedition members, completed their descent to basecamp and flew off the mountain on the 18th. Chen was evaluated at the 14,200-foot NPS camp and released while still suffering from exhaustion and mild AMS and residual effects of high altitude pulmonary edema. The Chen expedition recuperated for two days and completed their descent to basecamp.

HIGH ALTITUDE CEREBRAL EDEMA (HACE)
Alaska, Mount McKinley, West Buttress
The "Kiwi Denali" expedition included Richard Walshe, Andre Bell, Dave McKinley, and Pete O'Connor. On June 6 three of the members, including Walshe, Bell, and O'Connor, departed from the 17,200-foot camp en route to the summit via the West Buttress. During their ascent Bell separated from the group and descended to the group's camp at 17,200 feet by himself. Walshe and O'Connor, moving slower, continued and reached the summit by mid-afternoon. During their descent Walshe began to have difficulty walking. At

1630 an NPS patrol that had reached the summit ridge that afternoon caught up with Walshe and O'Connor during their descent. Ranger Michael Nash contacted the 14,200-foot NPS camp and relayed Walshe's condition.

Nash, his two patrol members, and O'Connor used short rope and running belay techniques to lower Walshe to Denali Pass. Walshe remained ataxic, stumbling and falling frequently, and was unable to care for himself during the three hour descent to Denali Pass. At Denali Pass an RMI guided group caught up with the lowering party and assisted with the traverse from the pass by setting additional anchors. At 2000 the NPS camp contacted several other guides located at the 17,200 feet and asked for assistance. Several guides ascended to the Denali Pass traverse and began setting fixed lines. Walshe was lowered down the fixed lines and arrived at 17,200 feet at 2400. Walshe was stabilized, evaluated, and found to be suffering from high altitude cerebral edema (HACE). Walshe was treated with Dexamethasone as per protocol, hydrated, and observed throughout the night. The following day, with the assistance of his three other expedition members, Walshe descended to the 14,200-foot camp where he was again evaluated and treated by NPS personnel. Walshe remained at 14,200 feet for 48 hours and completed the descent to basecamp with his team, returning to Talkeetna on June 19.

Analysis

Neither You or Walshe reported having AMS symptoms prior to their summit day making high altitude pulmonary edema and cerebral edema unpredictable factors with the potential to cause disaster in the high mountains. All groups were fortunate that climbers in the area were able to assist in the descent from 19,000 feet. (Source: Billy Shott, Mountaineering Ranger)

FALL INTO CREVASSE, EXCEEDING ABILITIES
Alaska, Mount McKinley, West Buttress

On the morning of July 5 at approximately 0100 the "Death March 2000" expedition left basecamp to begin a climb of Mount McKinley. At 0330 Kelly Thomas (35) fell into a crevasse on the main Kahiltna Glacier at 6,800 feet. Thomas initially fell only to his waist, at which point he removed his pack and pushed it away from him. He then fell into the crevasse a distance of approximately 30 feet. Thomas' partner, Tim Lapham (33), arrested the fall, set up an anchor and attempted to haul Thomas out. Thomas was unable to ascend due to improperly tying his ascension system into his harness prior to falling. Lapham could make very little progress due to the amount of rope drag in the system. At 0430 Lapham contacted Annie Duquette at basecamp via the CB radio and requested assistance. Ranger Meg Perdue was awakened by the radio traffic and requested more information from the team as to location and injuries. Lapham was unsure of his exact location, but stated the Kahiltna Glacier two hours out from basecamp. Thomas was apparently uninjured.

At 0445 Perdue contacted Daryl Miller and advised him of the situation. It was determined that Perdue and Jamail would prepare to leave on a ground rescue, Miller would assess the possibility for air ops support and call back within 30 minutes. At 0515, Miller called back that air ops were not possible due to weather conditions. Perdue was advised to go ahead with ground operations. At 0545 Perdue and Jamail left basecamp, where it was raining heavily with moderate winds. By 0700 they had reached the party and were assessing the situation. Perdue lowered a jacket to Thomas who was complaining of becoming cold and no longer shivering. Jamail and Perdue set up an anchor and 3:1 haul system on a separate rope, prepared a new lip and lowered a bight of rope to Thomas. Thomas clipped into this second rope and Jamail and Perdue were able to haul him out by 0730. By 0815 "Death March 2000" was heading back towards basecamp, arriving there at 1145.

Analysis

The major contributing factor to this incident was inexperience. The size of the party, the time they chose to climb, the way they had set up their rope system and subsequent rescue systems all point to an unfortunate lack of experience. The party had decided to attach two ropes together to increase the distance between them in the event of a crevasse fall, as a result they had approximately 150 feet between them. This became an impractical distance due to the amount of rope-drag if a haul system was needed and which left each of them carrying a coil of rope much too short to be useful. Though Lapham appeared to have set a reasonable anchor, the rope had cut so far into the lip of the crevasse that it should have been obvious that it would be impossible to haul his partner out. To this team's credit, they did show the good judgment to turn around once they realized the seriousness of the conditions they were encountering and decided to try their climb again another time. (Source: Meg Perdue, Mountaineering Ranger)

FALL ON ROCK, ROPE SEVERED BY FALLING ROCK
Alaska, Portage Glacier

I am sorry to report the death of Steve Garvey (40) on August 13. He was well known, experienced, and a much-liked Alaskan climber. Garvey, as he was known by all, was a friend of AMRG, a close personal friend, an occasional climbing partner and a seven-year employee of my company.

Garvey had completed a morning climb Friday with partner Matt Howard and was leading a second climb at noon when Howard noticed the safety rope go slack. Howard turned and saw Garvey hit the rock outcrop on which he was standing and roll a few feet down a shale slope. Garvey died when his rope was cut during a short leader fall. He fell over 100 feet to the ground.

Garvey was wearing a helmet and was briefly conscious after the fall. When his partner arrived at his side only seconds later, Garvey whispered, "What happened?" His face then quickly blanched and he lost consciousness. CPR efforts were ineffective and did not revive him. It appears Garvey had a flail chest among other internal injuries that may have caused massive internal bleeding and loss of blood pressure.

Analysis

Garvey was in the process of extending the upper limits of a route he had pioneered. His partner was familiar with the route he was climbing, and feels Garvey was possibly moving left horizontally six feet from an anchor to round a point on the route. A fall at this point would result in a short pendulum swing back below the previous anchor. Garvey's rope was only three weeks old. But it was cut in half only a foot from his harness.

The rocks on the route were on the side of a glacier carved valley, and were known for being sharp. Another employee of ours had climbed with Garvey in this area and remembers doing a route several years ago that incorporated an otherwise easy layback section that was unclimbable because the sharp rock edges sliced his fingers open. (Source: Bill Laxson, Alaska Mountain Rescue Group)

PROTECTION PULLED OUT WHEN WEIGHTED–FALL ON ROCK, TRYING TO STICK TO A SCHEDULE
California, Yosemite National Park, El Capitan

Craig (25) had several years of free climbing experience but little with aid. On May 29, he and his partners, Brent and Dave, decided to get some practice by climbing the first pitch (A3) of the Sea of Dreams, a Grade VI route on El Capitan.

Craig led 30–40 feet up a crack system a few feet right of a right facing corner, and placed a cam at his high point. The Sea of Dreams crack lay about 15 feet further right, with no way to climb across, so a pendulum was in order. He was able to place a small nut a couple of feet to his right, as a pivot point; then Brent lowered him from it until he could swing over to the route, where he clipped his etrier to a fixed copperhead and started up the crack.

Craig climbed two more fixed copperheads, putting him a little above the level of his pivot point, now 15 feet or so to his left. He didn't trust the fixed pieces so he hadn't clipped his rope through them, but the next placement looked solid. He top stepped his etrier and was about to place a piece when the copperhead supporting him blew out. He fell straight down and then pendulumed left, pulling out his pivot, the small nut. Brent and Dave watched as he continued swinging left, now supported by the cam. He smashed into the right facing corner with his right shoulder and then his helmet and went limp, but by the time Brent had lowered him 20 feet to the ground, he was beginning to regain consciousness. Dave ran down to the road to find someone with a cell phone.

The Park Service got the call at 7:15 p.m., and the first rescuers reached the scene 30 minutes later—about an hour after the accident. They immobilized Craig in a vacuum body splint and a litter, and carried him half a mile down the talus to the ambulance. It was well after dark now, but a med-evac helicopter was able to land at the park's heli base and fly Craig to a Fresno hospital, where he was treated for torn shoulder ligaments, a scalp laceration, and a concussion. His shoulder will take several months to heal. He still doesn't remember the copperhead failing or his collision with the wall, but he credits his helmet with preventing a serious head injury.

Analysis

Craig was concerned about a swinging fall, but wasn't able to place more protection across the traverse. At least he recognized the risk and made a conscious choice. Many climbers don't understand how dangerous even a short pendulum can be, especially when you strike a corner. Craig's case illustrates the problem: He hit the wall with approximately the same force as if he'd fallen an equal distance vertically to the ground, but instead of landing on his feet, he took the impact on his side.

Craig might have protected against the pendulum fall by adding a second belay line, as follows: He ties into their second rope. Dave (the third partner) belays him from a well anchored position, on the ground, to Craig's right (or places a solid directional at that point and belays from any position). This rope would not run through any of the primary rope's protection. (Source: John Dill, SAR Ranger)

FALL ON ROCK, INADEQUATE BELAY – ROPE TOO SHORT, INATTENTION
California, Yosemite Valley, Manure Pile Buttress

I'd like to say it was a cold, blustery, winter day and our heads were foggy and our brains numb from the bitter temperatures. And I'd like to blame that on our accident, but I can't. It was, in fact, May 25, a beautiful, warm and sunny day, and we had finished climbing After Six to the top of Manure Pile Buttress, quite pleased with ourselves.

We had enjoyed a shower and dinner and were headed to camp to meet friends when Marcus suggested we go back to Manure Pile for "one more climb" on the first pitch of After Seven (5.7). We had been eyeing the route for awhile, and were feeling heady after our day. I had reservations, because it was late and I was relaxed, but Marcus was feeling strong and I was easily swayed, being a bit feverish about the challenge, myself. What doubts I had I kept to myself as we drove to the climb.

Once at the base, he asked to go first. I positioned myself as belayer and watched as he skillfully and confidently led the pitch. The daylight was waning, and I really wanted my turn—I intended to practice placing pro with a top rope, so I told him, "Hurry up and come down so I can climb, too." I had no idea how quickly he would be heeding my words.

At the top of the climb, he set up a rappel and threw the rope down. I told him the rope ends didn't touch the ground. He said, "You'll have to belay me, then." Neither of us caught the ridiculous notion that our single 50-meter rope would somehow grow longer with me belaying rather than him rappelling.

I lowered him slowly, stopping him at each piece and watching intently as he cleaned his pro. When he was about 75 feet above me, he said, "Lower me faster," so I pulled the lever on the Gri-Gri. The end of the rope shot out of my hand, through the device, and flew up the wall. I shouted to Marcus to grab the pro, the rope, anything, but as he heard me, he began to fall, and there was no way to grab anything but air at that point.

I will never forget him falling as long as I live. It was like watching a slow motion movie: every nuance, every direction he turned, every spin of his foot-work, I saw with infinite clarity. I ran over to where he was falling and stood there with my arms stretched out. I have no idea what I was thinking. I'm sure it was simply a subconscious reaction. He began to pitch head first toward the ground and I just knew he was going to die. If my guts had sunk any lower, they would have been buried in the dirt.

I don't remember Marcus hitting the ground. I don't remember him hitting me, but I wound up on the ground, crawling over to him, and a deep bone bruise appeared on my arm two days later where he hit it. In fact my entire body was wracked, as if I had been torqued suddenly, in one big twisting mo-tion, by his impact.

I made sure Marcus had no problems breathing, then I ran out to the parking lot and got someone to call for help with a cell phone. The rescue team had Marcus out quickly and down to his own hospital in Modesto (where we both worked in the ER). Marcus was extremely lucky. He had fractured his right heel (a horrible fracture), two vertebrae, and his right elbow, and the skin had liter-ally shredded off of his hands as he tried to grab at anything while coming down. Thank God he never hit his head, because he was not wearing a helmet. He has recovered remarkably well, armed with a healthy body and a will of iron. He is ready to climb again, and can't wait to get back on the rock. I'm more spooked than he is, and amazingly enough, he wants to climb with me again!

Analysis

Marcus (33) and I (35) have been climbing for several years, although we have both been leading for only one season, at the 5.6–5.7 level. We are extremely safety conscious and always double check everything as we're setting up an-chors, before we rappel, etc., but we lacked experience retreating from longer single pitches. Ironically, we were going to take an intermediate rock course in the Valley the next day because we felt our ability to physically climb had out-stripped our knowledge of safety techniques.

Despite our careful attitude, a really horrible accident happened that could have easily been prevented. Had either of us recognized that the rope wasn't long enough, Marcus could have walked off the top. Had I tied a knot in the end of the rope, or tied myself to it, it wouldn't have gone through the Gri-Gri. Finally, I think that, on some level, our brains had turned off when we had eaten and showered, and then, racing against dark, tried to cram in one more pitch. If there is one lesson learned the hard way that applies to any sport, it's "When you're done, you're done."

I still feel foolish in telling this story. I thank God that Marcus is alive and well, although it was a long and painful recovery for him. His injury will un-doubtedly plague him on some level forever. I'm still quite skittish on the rock, and have had a rather prolonged mental recovery myself. It has changed both of us forever. If I could turn back time, I would in a heartbeat. (Source: Suzanne Johnson, MD)

(Editor's Note: Lest the reader think, "This will never happen to me," mistakes like this occur with climbers of all skills levels.)

STRANDED – WEATHER, INADEQUATE EQUIPMENT, HYPOTHERMIA
California, Yosemite Valley, Half Dome

English climbers Justin (28) and Luke (about 25) arrived in the Valley in May, intent on climbing the regular Northwest Face of Half Dome (24 pitches, VI 5.9 A2). On May 31 they hiked up the slab approach and climbed six pitches. By the next evening, they had reached Big Sandy Ledge (top of pitch 17). They were right on schedule, seven pitches from the summit, and expecting to top out the next day. The weather had been good and the rock dry to that point, but as they arrived at Big Sandy they were hit by a heavy, 45-minute rain shower.

They left Big Sandy the next morning at 6:00 a.m., aiming to reach the top by mid-afternoon. It had started to snow lightly, but they decided it would be easier to push on than to descend the route. However, they were slowed by worsening snow conditions, and when they arrived at the bottom of the last pitch—a 5.7 slab—they found it unclimbable because of a covering of verglas and snow. They spent some time looking for a way to aid around the impasse, but all the possibilities they could see eventually rejoined the slab—and the ice—before reaching the summit. It was getting dark, so they decided it would be safer to bivouac than to attempt to continue.

They found a spot out of the wind and shared their single bivy sack. They had deliberately left their sleeping bags at home in order to go light, but had brought storm jackets and pants, and plenty of warm clothes, including mittens and hats. This gear had kept them comfortable so far.

There was little or no water running on the rock at their bivy that night, but the temperature was just below freezing, and their own body heat melted the snow that fell on them. Their bivy sack was made completely of a waterproof, breathable material, without a coated nylon bottom. The snow melt leaked through the sack into their clothes and even ran down their necks.

They spent a miserable night, and by the morning of June 3, they were wet, cold, and completely covered by snow. They considered rappelling, but the route had wandered so much that it would be difficult to reverse and would expose them further to the weather. They decided to wait for the sun to melt the ice off the slab, figuring they'd be able to summit by mid-afternoon. But it stayed cloudy and cold, reducing them to blowing a whistle in hopes of attracting hikers on the summit; whether no one was there or the sound didn't carry, they got no response. Another bivouac was likely, whether they tried to descend or wait out the weather. They would survive another night, but thought they would not be able to function on their own the next day.

At about 7 a.m. on the 3rd, Mark, an acquaintance who had been a day ahead of them on the route, notified the NPS that Justin and Luke were overdue. He thought that they would have been down already if they had retreated because of the storm.

The overdue party was not visible from the Valley floor, but the clouds were breaking up, and the NPS helicopter quickly found them. By the time the rescue team was able to land on the summit and lower a rescuer, both climbers were hypothermic, with frost nip on their hands and feet. Despite their condition, they managed to climb the rescue team's ropes to the summit.

Analysis

Justin and Luke had experience in stormy alpine weather and knew that storms were common in Yosemite, but they had not expected to encounter ice on the summit slabs. ("Staying Alive," the safety chapter in the Yosemite climbing guide, which they had read, states, "Temperatures may drop, freezing solid the next pitch...") May and June bring plenty of serious storms in the park, and any face climbing pitch may become impassable due to water or ice. Half Dome is particularly prone to winter conditions. At 8842 feet, its summit rises almost a mile above the Valley floor. The weather is equivalent to that in the high country, with occasional blizzards, ice—and rescues—even in August.

Claims of waterproof breathable fabric (Goretex and other brands) leaking, whether true or not, are common among wall climbers. Even with coated nylon bottoms, bivy sacks are notoriously poor shelters in wet conditions. There are just too many ways for water to find its way inside. The closest thing to a fool-proof shelter is a well designed portaledge in good condition, with properly sealed seams.

Two factors aided their survival. First, and most important, friends knew where they were. Second, the clouds broke enough for the NPS to fly. A ground approach—an eight-mile uphill hike in the snow—would have taken the rescue team several more hours, leaving Justin and Luke on the wall into the next night. (Source: John Dill, NPS Ranger, Yosemite National Park)

FALL ON ROCK, INADEQUATE PROTECTION, PROTECTION PULLED OUT, OVERCONFIDENCE
California, Yosemite Valley, El Capitan

Dave and I (Rob) had been planning to climb the Nose of El Cap (34 pitches, Grade VI, 5.11, A2) for the past year. Together we had 24 years of climbing experience, including many traditional 5.10 and 5.11 leads and a couple of Yosemite walls, so we felt the climbing would be challenging, but easily within our limits. I had not been climbing much in the last four years, so I had intended to climb outdoors as much as possible during our year of preparation. However, innumerable projects at work consumed nearly all my time. All I could manage were a couple of hours per week in a climbing gym and one weekend at Joshua Tree, where I did lots of 5.10 cracks. So my prep for the ascent hadn't gone as planned, but I still felt physically strong from the gym. Also, this was the first time in fifteen years that I could take a vacation at the right time of year, so I wanted to go for it. I thought that a few warm-up routes in the Valley would get me back to feeling totally comfortable on granite.

Rushing to tie up loose ends at work shrank my two week vacation to a week and a half. We arrived in Yosemite in the middle of a June storm. A cold biting wind, and rain and snow marked our first two days there. The Nose is often crowded, and friends had described it as a "bowling alley" with falling rocks and equipment funneling onto lower parties. But there seemed to be nobody up there except for one group braving the storm on El Cap Tower. We'd already lost some climbing days due to work and the weather, and here was the opportunity to do the route with only one party above us, so we changed our plans. We would skip the warm-up routes and jump on the Nose as soon as the storm broke.

On June 3, our third day in the Valley, the weather was still nasty but the prediction was good, so we decided to get started. We got to the base at midday, a little later than we wanted. Another party must have been listening to the forecast; they were just starting the first pitch when we arrived, but they were fixing ropes to Sickle Ledge (top of pitch 4) and starting up from the ground the next morning. Our plan was not to fix, but to climb to Sickle and bivy there. Since both parties climbed at comparable speeds, we thought we could pretty much stay out of each other's way on the route.

We got to Sickle Ledge later than expected, after dark, so I had a quick dinner and fixed the next 60-meter section (pitches 5 and 6) by headlamp. By the time I returned to Sickle, reorganized the gear, and got into my sleeping bag it was well past midnight. Morning came way too soon. The sounds of the other party jugging their lines and a new party starting the route woke us up well after dawn, about 8:00 a.m. I was still tired.

We ate a quick breakfast, and Dave jugged up the line and hauled our gear. I stayed behind to control the haul bag with a back rope, so by the time I started up, the party below was jugging their last rope, right on our heels. I was carrying a pack, unbalanced at that, so the last steep part up to Dave was tiring, and I arrived at the anchors out of breath. In an effort to save time. I decided to take the whole rack with me on the next pitch. Since the climbing was rated at only 5.8, I thought the extra weight wouldn't be much of a problem.

Pitch 7 started with a long tension traverse. After being lowered 30–40 feet, I worked my way toward the next corner system to the right. Frictioning out on tension, I realized that my brand new shoes didn't provide the foot sensitivity that I am comfortable with. They were my usual model, but they weren't broken in and the soles were thick and not scuffed. I hadn't noticed it much the day before because we had aided most of the way to Sickle.

Once I reached the corner, the climbing was only 5.6 and I quickly made it to an old, bolted belay station, 30 feet to Dave's right and horizontal with him. I didn't want the lead rope to go straight right from Dave and then make a 90-degree bend to follow me up the pitch, so I skipped clipping the bolts and climbed higher. The climbing was still easy and I was feeling confident and moving quickly. The hand-sized crack above looked good.

I got to a point where the angle of the rope looked okay and placed my first piece, a cam. I estimate I was now 30 feet to Dave's right and 15 feet above him. I considered placing more gear here, but I wanted to save time and keep our hand-sized cams for what looked like the crux above and possibly for the belay, still a long way up. I climbed another 15 feet or so, where the wall steepened to vertical and the crack narrowed to thin hands. Though I was still below the crux, it wasn't the best of all stances—I had a right hand jam and the tip of my right foot in the crack, not really solid—but I decided to stop and place another cam.

My first choice was slightly too small. The long layoff from climbing put me a little out of practice. Also the rack was huge, so it took longer than usual to find the right size. Although the stance had been adequate for a short stay, I was getting more fatigued by the second, the weight of the rack getting heavier and heavier. After digging through the hardware, I found the right cam and placed it. My hand was beginning to sweat. I reached down to grab the rope and clip the 'biner when, Boom!, my foot popped out of the crack and I was falling.

Everything happened fast: I tried to grab the rock, but it was going by too quickly. I never felt the cam, but it must have pulled out, since I kept going farther and farther, gaining more and more speed. The sound of the air rushing by me was intense. There were lots of little impacts, not hard, but I'd let out a grunt each time. Then I hit something and flipped over and the back of my head struck the rock. My helmet absorbed the brunt of the impact, but now I was falling upside down, incredibly fast; a head first blow, I was thinking, would surely snap my neck. When the rope caught, I was jerked left in a huge pendulum, still hitting the wall, 50–60 feet below Dave. I swung around the corner into the right facing dihedral we'd come from, and finally stopped there. The math works out to a 70-foot vertical fall plus the high speed pendulum.

At first, everything seemed to be okay. I could feel and move my hands and feet, and I just felt badly bruised, with the wind knocked out of me. But I couldn't raise my arms, and, although the pain hadn't set in at that point, I thought I had broken both shoulders. I called up to Dave to see if he was all right. He said his hand had jammed in the ATC while holding my fall; it was swelling and might be broken.

After a while, Dave got things sorted to the point where he could lower me to Sickle. It wasn't easy, because I had to get down through all the blocks in the dihedral without my hands, using only my butt and legs. The party on Sickle helped out any way they could; one was a Wilderness First Responder and Dave was an EMT B, and they constantly checked me over for head injuries.

Initially I thought that I could continue lowering to the ground with everyone's help. But my shoulders had started to hurt about 30 minutes after the fall, and the pain gradually became excruciating. I felt completely immobile—any movement, even breathing, intensified the pain. The last thing I wanted to do was to call for a rescue, but I soon relented, and one of the guys rapped to the trail to get help.

The NPS got the word a little before 10:00 a.m. Two YOSAR climbers came up the fixed lines and two rangers rappelled out of the park helicopter. They thoroughly checked me over and came to the conclusion that I had probably dislocated both shoulders. They couldn't rule out spine or shoulder fractures, however, so they immobilized me in a spine splint. Clouds had been building on the rim all morning, and the wind had picked up to the point where it was too dangerous for the park helicopter to extricate me, but the bigger Huey from Lemoore Naval Air Station arrived just before noon to back up the NPS. The

Navy helicopter hoisted me off Sickle with no problem, saving me a long lower down the wall and a potentially bumpy carryout on the trail—though the rangers said that if we'd gone that route I'd be floating on a cloud of morphine.

The physician at the Yosemite clinic found that Dave's hand was only bruised, and that my injuries were two dislocated shoulders, a hairline crack in the left one, and a whole lot of bruises. About eight hours after my fall, they reduced the dislocations and I was able to ride home with Dave. I had to let the shoulders heal for six weeks before starting physical therapy; they're still really weak seven months later, but I've started going to the gym.

Analysis

A lot of factors contributed to my accident, not the least of which was inadequate protection. After a long tension traverse like that, I like to at least double up the first piece because of the long runout and because the angle of the rope can create a sideways pull on the protection, making it more likely to "walk out"—which is what I suspect happened.

Instead I relied on just one piece and spent too little time placing it because a) I felt pressure to stay ahead of the party below, b) I wanted to get back on schedule by reaching El Cap Tower early, c) it was still easy going, and d) I thought I would soon have many additional pieces up higher. The cam seemed solid and oriented for an out and down pull, so I quickly moved on, instead of making absolutely sure it was bombproof.

Since I wasn't all that high above Dave vertically, I had the illusion that I wasn't running it out, but with the rope making a bend and the pendulum factored in there, I really was. It may have been better to just clip the bolts for my first protection, regardless of the angle—they're multi directional.

Another factor was my failure to break in the shoes. I've done many "R" and a couple of "X" rated leads. I normally know when I am on the verge of falling, so, if I'm placing protection, I'll readjust my stance if necessary. Although I was getting fatigued, I didn't realize my foot was about to pop because I couldn't feel much in those new shoes.

But the shoes were a minor problem, because if I had concentrated better I could have easily adjusted my stance. The main factor was my preparation, both mental and physical. Four years ago most 5.8 cracks posed little or no challenge, even when I was weighed down with a full rack and a backpack. The warm up climbs in the Valley should have been mandatory, as a way of assessing my present climbing abilities. Gym climbing kept me physically strong, but my friction footwork suffered and it was not adequate preparation for the type of climbing on this route. The gym and the 5.10s at Joshua Tree just made me overconfident.

Being immobilized by pain was scary, and I was lucky that YOSAR was there to bail me out. What if this had been in the backcountry? If we had brought prescription strength pain medication along, we might have been able to self rescue with the help of the other party. Reducing the dislocations soon after the injury might also be an option, especially in a remote situation. Some people have "trick" shoulders that they can pop back in easily, but most dislocations are more serious; reducing them requires training and present a risk of complications, especially if shoulder fractures are involved. A Wilderness First Responder course provides the training to decide when and how to attempt a reduction; it's now high on my list of things to do. (Source: Rob S. and John Dill, NPS Ranger, Yosemite National Park)

FALLING ROCK
California, Yosemite Valley, Glacier Point Apron
After climbing in the Valley for a couple of weeks, Peter Terbush (22), Joseph Kewin (21), and Kerry Pyle (20) were nearing the end of their vacation. On June 13, in late afternoon, they decided to climb Apron Jam, a one pitch, 5.9 crack near the west end of Glacier Point Apron. Pyle led the pitch while Terbush belayed at the base and Kewin lounged beside him.

Just after 7:30 p.m., as Pyle was finishing the pitch, he heard a loud rumble above, and, within a second or two, boulders the size of Volkswagens were flying by to his right. He scrambled the last few feet to the belay (a pair of bolts), clipped in two quickdraws, and began forming a clove hitch in his rope, as a tie in. Before he could finish, rock fragments slammed into his head. He dropped the rope and simply grabbed the quickdraws and pressed himself against the wall. He grew faint and nauseous from the blows but hung on and survived. Without a helmet, he received severe scalp lacerations, but no other major injuries. As the rockfall ceased, he noticed that his lead rope was still snug, and called down to his friends. Kewin responded that he was OK but that Terbush might be dead.

When the rockfall began, Kewin scrambled several feet east to get out of the way, and, like Pyle, hugged the wall. After the noise stopped, he went back to Terbush and found him unresponsive and pulseless. Terbush had not moved from his original position; in fact, he was still holding Pyle's rope as if on belay. Kewin removed the rope from Terbush's hands so that Pyle could use it to rappel, then he ran down to the parking lot for help. One ranger arrived a few minutes later and confirmed that Terbush had received fatal head injuries.

The NPS delayed bringing Terbush out until it could assess the risk of more rockfall. On the 14th, NPS and USGS specialists examined the release point by helicopter and telescope; despite a couple of very small rockfalls that day, they permitted a ground team to make the recovery on the 15th.
Analysis
The rockfall that killed Terbush—estimated at 525 tons—originated 1200 feet up the Apron, just above the Oasis, and fell directly down the Harding route. Terbush, Kewin, and Pyle were 300–500 feet left of the main fall, yet unfortunately within range of the shrapnel. The same release point has been active since at least November 1998, when an even bigger fall occurred that sent small rocks as far as the tents at Camp Curry. (For a detailed geological report on this series of rockfalls, go to http://landslides.usgs.gov/html_files/landslides/newsinfo.shtml)

Large rockfalls occur in the valley almost every year. However, with granite walls so steep and fractured, it's surprising that there aren't more. In fact, almost all rockfall related climbing injuries and deaths are from single rocks pulled off by the victims or other climbers nearby, rather than from spontaneous releases.

Peter Terbush was not anchored, so he may have had a brief opportunity to unclip the ATC from his harness and run for cover. We'll never know his thoughts or intentions, but he did know that his partner was still on belay. Whether deliberate or instinctive, he stayed put, maintaining that belay at the expense of his own safety. It's fitting that his friends have nominated him for the Carnegie Medal for Heroism. (Source: John Dill, NPS Ranger, Yosemite National Park)

FALLING ROCK, NO HARD HAT
California, Kings Canyon National Park, North Dome

In mid-June, we—Brandon Thau (23), Matthew Pollard (24), and Jennifer Pollard (25)—completed a new route up North Dome, topping out around 4:00 p.m. The climb had involved hanging bivouacs. After repacking the bags, we started our descent. We started heading in the direction of the descent gully, but it was slow going with Grade VI haul bags. We were forced to bivy. We didn't have much food, but had plenty of water.

We started the next day by scouting for the best way to achieve the descent gully with minimal rappels and exposure. With the burden of large packs, we were forced to do a handful of short rappels. It was during one of these rappels that the accident occurred.

Before every rappel, we would clear the loose rocks and debris from the area around the rope and anchor to minimize the risk of falling rocks while we rappelled. After the third rappel, I dropped my pack and hiked up a little to reduce rope drag when I pulled them. I don't remember how much—if any— of the rope I pulled before a rock whacked me in the head. I was on a little ledge and when the rock hit me, I went flying—and began yelling. A plethora of small bushes cushioned my landing. Brandon and Jennifer heard me. Brandon immediately started running to help me while Jennifer went for the first aid kit. While Brandon was scrambling up to me, he was asking me my name, his name, my birthday, where we were, if I could feel my fingers and toes, if I could see him clearly. Luck was on my side, because I could answer all those questions correctly.

There was a lot of blood, but direct pressure stopped the bleeding, and it was determined that I only had a flesh wound. I was able to scramble down to the packs by myself. After dressing the laceration, the bandage was held in place by my helmet. I descended without a pack, letting Brandon and Jennifer shuttle the gear. About an hour after the incident, I felt strong enough to carry my pack. We arrived at our cars about 4:00 p.m.

Analysis

Be skeptical of descents that you do not have first-hand knowledge of. Take your time—even if it means putting down the packs and scouting.

Even though we took utmost care to clear away potentially dangerous rocks from the rappel anchors, we didn't follow our own rule of wearing helmets. All three of us wore them on the ascent. Why not the descent? We assumed the descent was going to be safe and worry free. After all, we have been rappelling since the first day we climbed! The damage would surely have been less if my helmet had been on my head rather than in my pack.

The final take-home message is to be ready for accidents. Be familiar with first aid and always carry a first aid kit—or know how to improvise if the unfortunate situation arises whereby you are the one between your partner and the Grim Reaper. (Source: Edited from a report submitted by Matthew Pollard)

FALL ON ROCK – MISJUDGED PENDULUM
California, Yosemite Valley, El Capitan

On June 28, Mario (42), Peter (30), and Gilbert (40), all from Austria, were in their second day on the Nose (34 pitches, VI 5.11 A2), and preparing to make the King Swing—the long pendulum left from Boot Flake (pitch 18). Peter led across, followed by Gilbert. Mario let out the haulbag, and then it was his turn to follow.

Mario's pendulum rope led left to where Peter and Gilbert waited at the next belay. As he rappelled on his back rope down the left side of the Boot (a boot-shaped flake roughly one half pitch in length), the pendulum rope began taking his weight and swinging him slowly to the left. When he thought he had swung far enough across, he released one end of his back rope, letting it pull through its anchor. No longer restrained by this rope, he expected to continue swinging gently left on his pendulum rope until he was directly below his partners.

Mario quickly found that he had underestimated the remaining distance and, therefore, the speed of his swing. Furthermore, the wall here is not flat, but dips into a shallow open book hiding a corner that he hadn't expected. Striking the corner started him spinning. As his pendulum continued, he reached out to the wall with his left hand to stop the spin, but the impact on his arm broke both bones in his forearm near the wrist.

His partners lowered him several meters to a ledge. Then Peter came down, examined the wrist, wrapped it with an elastic bandage and gave him some pain medication.

Mario claimed that he had not hit his torso or his head and had not been unconscious. However, the distracting pain in his wrist had made him seem confused for a few minutes, so his friends were worried that he might not be aware of internal injuries. They felt they should not risk rappelling to the ground with him (about 1500 feet, with more than a dozen rappels and several hanging belays), so one partner rappelled alone with two of their three ropes, thinking that would be the quickest way to get help.

The reporting party contacted the NPS at approximately 12:30 p.m., stating his concern that Mario may have been briefly unconscious. Several rescue team members were flown to the summit in the NPS helicopter while others, using a loudspeaker and telescope from the Valley floor, confirmed that Mario was currently conscious and alert. Nevertheless, the NPS requested a hoist equipped UH 1N Huey helicopter from Lemoore Naval Air Station. If his partner's concern proved true and Mario's condition worsened, the Huey would be able to hoist him directly from the wall. (Because the helicopter's rotor blades would have to be fairly close to the cliff at that location, NPS flight safety policies precluded a direct helicopter approach unless Mario began to show evidence of a more serious injury.)

The summit team lowered a Park Medic about 1500 feet to the scene. She confirmed that Mario's injury appeared limited to his forearm and that he could be hoisted by his harness, without a litter. The Navy aircraft was released from the rescue. Rescuer and patient were hauled to the top and flown down to the Yosemite clinic just before dark, where Mario's fractures were confirmed. (Nine months later, his wrist still lacked its normal range of motion and will probably require further surgery.)

Analysis

Mario was very experienced and had dealt with pendulum traverses before. In this case he simply misjudged his speed. Whenever possible, let yourself across the traverse under complete control, until you are fully supported by the next anchor.

Mario's party may not have realized that, with El Capitan's excellent acoustics, yelling for help is often faster than rappelling.

In hindsight, Mario could probably have descended the wall with his partners. Since they were right on the Nose rappel route, this may have gotten him down faster than the NPS could have rescued him. However, his partners' concerns about internal injuries were reasonable, and moving him themselves may have worsened a hidden injury. It can be a difficult decision to make; but the self rescue option may be mandatory in a more remote setting. (Source: John Dill, NPS Ranger, Yosemite National Park)

(Editor's Note: For more about pendulums, see CA incidents on May 29 and June 4 in this issue of ANAM, and also Coe, Half Dome, in ANAM 1998.)

ILLNESS – HACE, EXCEEDING ABILITIES, ASCENDING TOO FAST
California, Mount Shasta, Misery Hill

On July 30, Ken Goldstein (25) had stopped to rest at the base of Misery Hill (13,000 feet) and was later discovered unconscious and unresponsive. USFS climbing rangers were summoned. They administered oxygen to him, as he had regained consciousness. Goldstein was evacuated by a California Air National Guard helicopter and treated for HACE and dehydration at hospital. He recovered, but had no recollection of events surrounding the episode.

Analysis

Goldstein ascended too rapidly. Even at this elevation, one can develop serious altitude illness. (Source: Dan Tower, Wilderness Ranger, and Bob Musgrove.)

FALL ON ROCK, PROTECTION PULLED OUT
California, Yosemite Valley, El Capitan

In the afternoon of September 9, Russ Fields (29), Bob Dunahue (36), and Bill Hesse (27) reached Long Ledge on the Salathe Wall (35 pitches, Grade VI).

Russ had the next lead, pitch 33; the topo shows it starting as A1, then finishing as 5.8 face climbing.

Comfortable on hard 5.10, he didn't expect any problems, but about 50 feet short of the belay, he found the free moves much harder than the rating. He searched for an easier way, found nothing, and finally fell attempting the moves. His last protection, six or seven feet below, was a marginal placement—all he'd been able to find—and it failed. He was caught by the next piece after falling 25 to 30 feet—a clean fall, until his right foot struck a knob.

His partners got up the pitch, and Russ was able to follow the remaining pitches to the summit by jumaring on his good leg. As they topped out, they met two Yosemite SAR team members on a search assignment; the searchers stayed with them that night and arranged for the NPS helicopter to evacuate Russ in the morning. X-rays confirmed that his right ankle had been fractured.

Analysis

According to local climbers, this pitch is significantly underrated. There have been several other falls on it this year, and rumors of a few injuries, though none requiring a rescue. (Source: John Dill, NPS Ranger, Yosemite National Park)

(Editor's Note: It has become more common to rely on ratings from guide books rather than on one's own ability to judge the difficulty of a route. The latter is becoming a lost skill—along with being able to down-climb once the realization that the route won't go has set in.)

FALL ON HARD SNOW – UNABLE TO SELF ARREST, PARTY SEPARATED, EXCEEDING ABILITIES
California, Mount Shasta, Hotlum/Bolum Ridge

On September 12, a team of four climbers was descending the Hotlum/Bolum Ridge. Two of the team went ahead to scout the descent route. One member, Rene "Red" Arnold Cuestas (32), did not return. After waiting an hour, the three remaining team members continued to descend. When they returned to basecamp, Cuestas was not there, so they contacted USFS rangers. During the ensuing search, a California Division of Forestry and Fire helicopter crew spotted Cuestas' body at 12,000 feet. He appeared to have slipped on the ice and fallen two to three hundred feet over ice and rock. He was wearing crampons and had an ice ax girth hitched to his wrist.

Analysis

Cuestas was a novice climber. The route he was on is not technically difficult when snow conditions are good. However, the route generally becomes quite icy in the fall, making it very challenging. The party continued to climb, even though they were frightened by the conditions on the ascent. Separating on the descent may have contributed to the incident. (Source: Dan Towner, Wilderness Ranger, and Bob Musgrove)

FALL ON ROCK, PROTECTION PULLED, EXCEEDING ABILITIES
California, Yosemite Valley, Middle Cathedral Rock

On October 10, Dan Goriesky (43) set out to lead Pee Pee Pillar (a one pitch,

5.10a) with his friends Josh Vendig and Randy Dewees. The rating was just above Dan's comfort level, but the pitch was easily protected, and he had been solid on a couple of 10a's the day before.

Dan climbed 40–50 feet up a series of cracks to the start of the thin layback that leads to the belay. He placed several pieces along the way, the last two being a #7 wired stopper near the base of the layback and a similar sized Wallnut a foot or two higher. He was concerned about the top piece but feeling good about the climb, so he continued up.

When his feet were 4–5 feet above the top piece Dan felt them start to slip, and before he could reposition them, he was off. At first he fell upright, but his feet struck something that turned him on his back, horizontal. He felt and heard gear pulling out, and, after falling 20 feet, he struck the top of a pedestal with his lower back and pelvis. He bounced off, fell another 15–20 feet and was finally stopped by the belay, three feet above a ledge and 10–12 feet above the ground. Josh and Randy said he was hanging in a horizontal, slightly head down position, at that point.

Dan was conscious but complained of pain in his back. Josh lowered him to the ground while Randy guided him down, and someone nearby called the NPS by cell phone. The SAR team arrived 20 minutes later, immobilized his spine, and carried him in a litter a short distance down to the road. The clinic staff found he had escaped with nothing more than a lower back contusion, and he has fully recovered.

Analysis

The top piece had pulled out. The next one, a foot or so lower, was still in place, but the rope had unclipped from the carabiner, leaving a piece ten feet lower to stop Dan's fall. He is pretty sure he didn't grab the protection as he fell, so the most likely explanation for the rope unclipping is that it flipped over the carabiner's gate as he went by; the rope can then press down on the gate, opening it and allowing the rope to slip out. This is easy to demonstrate if you hold a carabiner in your hand, although it implies that Dan's carabiner may have been held in position against the rock somehow, despite being on a flexible quickdraw. Some leaders carry a couple of locking carabiners for such critical placements, although you can also use two regular carabiners—with gates properly reversed.

More surprising was the appearance of the carabiner after the fall: Instead of the gate swinging shut against the nose in the normal fashion, the tip of the gate had somehow swung past the nose and was now "outside" the carabiner. One possibility is that the force of the fall stretched the carabiner lengthwise; however, the body of the 'biner did not seem to be distorted. More likely, according to Chris Harmston, Black Diamond's quality assurance engineer, is that the rope forced the gate sideways as it pulled out of the 'biner. This can slightly distort the hinge fork on the gate, allowing the gate to pass to one side of the nose as it swings shut. No stretching of the body of the carabiner is necessary, and the gate can appear almost normal afterward, but with a slightly looser hinge. (Dan's carabiner was a Kong Bonaiti, bentgate with keylock, 22kN gate closed strength,

7 kN gate open strength.) Note that the "sprung" gate, while interesting, is more likely a *result* of the rope unclipping rather than the cause.

Dan was not wearing a helmet. He covered his head with his hands as he fell, and they took a pretty good blow. Helmets are more commonly worn on long climbs, but falls like this can happen anywhere. (Source: John Dill, NPS Ranger, Yosemite National Park)

FALL ON ROCK, INADEQUATE PROTECTION – KNOT PULLED THROUGH BOLT HANGER
California, Yosemite Valley, El Capitan

On October 27, Jim Fisher (30) and I, Scott Earnest (27), set out to climb Lurking Fear (20 pitches, VI 5.10 A3), our first El Cap route. We reached Thanksgiving Ledge in the afternoon of the 27th, and I began leading pitch 18.

The pitch was 5.10a, near my free climbing limit, but it went smoothly; after 100 feet or so I got to a single hangerless bolt where I thought the end of the pitch should be. But then I looked around and saw obvious belay bolts 15–20 feet to my left and 5–10 feet lower, and I realized that I was off route. I should have angled left during the pitch instead of climbing straight up.

I could have set up a good anchor and belayed right where I was, but I thought the hauling would be a pain because of the angle between Jim and me, so I decided to move over to those belay bolts. Free climbing across looked a little sketchy; instead, I opted to drop down and pendulum over to a crack where I could get in a piece and make a couple of easy moves up to the belay.

I yelled down to Jim to clip a bolt hanger on the haul line, and I pulled it up. It was a keyhole type that I could just slip over the nut and pull down to secure it for a downward pull. Instead of clipping a 'biner directly into the hanger, I rigged the hanger like a sky hook: I tied the tails of a piece of 5 mm cord together with an overhand knot, and stuffed the loop through the hanger from top to bottom so that the knot would keep the loop from pulling through. Then I clipped the rope to the loop under the hanger with a 'biner.

Jim lowered me. The route up had wandered, so I'd used some long slings to cut the rope drag, but I still had to push myself down the wall as Jim let out the line. I cleaned out a couple of pieces as I went, to reduce the drag. When I was down about 20 feet I made the swing—about 45 degrees; I missed the first try but ran harder the second time, got my fingers in the crack, my feet smeared on the wall, and leaned back against the rope to brace myself. I was pretty solid.

I was looking at the rack to see what cam I could pop in when I heard this "bink!" sound, and I looked up and saw big loops of the rope falling toward me. I've heard all kind of things rip out of the rock, but I'd never heard a sound like that, kind of like nylon breaking. In the half second before I started to fall, I thought "Oh my God, the rope broke." I was sure of it at the time, but the rope was fine and we discovered later that the knot in the 5mm cord had simply pulled through the hole in the hanger.

Because I'd back cleaned some pieces, the next protection was a chockstone

25 feet or more below the bolt, so I had at least 45 feet of slack. I only remember the first couple of seconds as I was falling. Jim says I smashed my head into a sloping ledge and stopped 10 feet above the belay, unconscious and upside down. I'd fallen roughly 70 feet, and the sling on the chockstone had caught me.

Jim anchored me off, got out of the belay, and was able to stand on a boulder to reach me and get me upright; then he went back to the belay and lowered me to the ledge.

I still don't remember any of that—after a couple of minutes I started waking up and the next thing I knew, I was sitting on Thanksgiving Ledge. Jim was standing over me, on the phone, and when I finally figured out who he was I said, "Hey Jim, what's going on? Where are we?" And he said, "You had a bad fall, man. We're on El Cap. You're going to be all right." And it started coming back. But then I saw my right arm, which was all deformed, and I started yelling, but Jim screamed back at me, "Calm down, it's just sprained." And I was still so out of it that I believed him.

This was the last steep pitch, so Jim briefly considered leading off, but abandoned that idea because I was still disoriented. He tried reaching the 911 operator and had no luck, but he finally got his own phone service carrier back in Denver, who patched him through to the NPS. It was a little after 4:30 p.m.

Two park rangers rappelled directly to us from their helicopter at 6:00 p.m. It was too close to dark to fly me off so the four of us bivouacked on Thanksgiving Ledge. By that time I was alert but had a mild headache, a big bruise on my forehead, and I was sore all over, with a lot of pain in my wrist. The rangers gave me little doses of morphine, which helped. It rained that night, but the weather cleared in the morning so the helicopter was able to short haul me straight off the ledge.

My helmet had absorbed part of the blow to my head, but I still wound up with twelve facial fractures, including my nose, cheeks, eye sockets, and forehead, and I had a minor amount of bleeding in my brain. I also fractured both bones in my forearm and was covered with lacerations. I've made almost a full recovery, except that I've lost about 30% of my sense of taste and smell because of nerve damage.

Analysis

Obviously, I should have had a bulkier knot or a thicker cord in the hanger, or just used a carabiner instead. We'd used the same hanger and cord rig all the way up the climb, but only for body weight, clipping directly to it for aid moves. With the rope running freely through the 'biner, and me hanging on the other side, I was putting closer to twice my weight on it (the pulley effect), and pushing myself down the wall and swinging around, in addition.

Furthermore, I should have backed up the bolt with something else. I was relying on the protection I'd placed before reaching the bolt, but I was too busy concentrating on the pendulum to realize that I had left myself open to a big fall by back cleaning those pieces. I wasn't concerned enough, because I assumed the bolt was bombproof and wasn't thinking about the hanger setup.

The helmet probably saved my life. It didn't prevent all my head injuries, because I hit partly on my face, but it obviously took a good whack because the internal harness had ripped partially loose from the shell.

Finally, our cell phone got help fast, but that's no reason to be careless. It's better to climb as if you had left it at home. (Source: Scott Earnest and John Dill, NPS Ranger, Yosemite National Park)

RAPPEL ERROR – UNEVEN ROPE ENDS, FALL ON ROCK
High Eagle Dome, Shuteye Ridge, California

On October 31, after setting up a toprope, I (45) tossed down it down and rappelled. About two thirds of the way down the route, I saw one taped end of the rope slipping through my rappel device, an image I will remember forever. I fell 20–25 feet to a broad, relatively flat granite ledge below.

I was in immediate pain and slightly amnesiac, did not lose consciousness. My right pelvis and leg were extremely painful, and I was unable to bear any weight on that leg. I was bleeding from a cut in my scalp. My partner, Nancy Bleile, a physician, quickly assessed my medical condition, then ran to catch up with friends who had just left to drive home. They returned and assisted in my evacuation. The evacuation to the car required about two hours, compared to an approach time of about 20 minutes.

Subsequent medical evaluation revealed four fractures: one in the sacrum and three in the transverse processes (bumps on the sides) of my lumbar vertebrae.

Analysis

I failed to bring the rope to its midway point before starting to rappel. I have climbed quite a bit over the past twelve years, and I read ANAM, so I am well aware that rappelling is a dangerous aspect of the sport. I generally double check the rappel system before starting down, and in this instance I double checked my harness buckle, the gear placements, and carabiner positions. But I forgot to even out the ends of the rope.

There was no good excuse for this mistake, but several things may have contributed to my haste. This was to be our last climb of the day, and as the sun began to sink in the sky, we could feel the late afternoon chill beginning to move in. Gear placements were somewhat hard to find, and I had to tinker to get solid placements. As I built the anchor and set up the rope, I was in a rather uncomfortable position. I was eager to get down and try the climb. The rope was moderately tangled, so I tossed it down, hoping it would straighten itself out.

Knotting the ends of the rope would have prevented the accident, though we had just done a nearby climb and we knew there was plenty of rope to reach the ground, had it been evened out. Or a partner on the ground, observing the toprope setup, could have stopped me before I got into trouble.

Had I rolled off the ledge, I might have fallen several hundred feet further. Had I landed differently, I might have sustained even more serious back or head injuries. I was not wearing a helmet, but I will be much more likely to do so in the future. (Source: Sam Gitchel)

STRANDED – DID NOT CHECK FIXED ROPES, DEHYDRATION, FATIGUE, WEATHER
California, Yosemite Valley, Lost Arrow Spire

Late fall in the Sierra Nevada had been mild, so in mid-December, Art (23), Robert (28), and Eric (22), all Yosemite locals, decided to climb the Direct Route on Lost Arrow Spire (13 pitches, VI 5.11 A3). They would finish in the notch between the Arrow and the main wall, roughly 300 feet below the rim. There is no enjoyable way to climb out, so it's customary to fix ropes from the rim into the notch as an escape. Art had been down to the notch before, when climbing the Arrow Spire, so he knew where to set up; on December 13, he and Eric hiked up the Yosemite Falls Trail with the gear. Art anchored one rope, tied another onto its free end, and threw them over the edge. Then he looked from a viewpoint on the rim to confirm that the rope reached all the way down to the notch.

On the 15th, the party of three fixed two pitches and slept at the base of the wall. The next day they climbed their lines and completed four more pitches, then dropped down to bivouac on the First Error, a ledge at the top of pitch 4.

They'd planned on two days for the climb and had brought along 8–12 liters of water—they're not sure how much. But they'd used some of it fixing pitches and found themselves working hard in hot, sunny weather, drinking more than they'd intended. That night they realized they were low on water. They briefly considered retreating, but figured they could stretch their supplies to the notch, then climb their fixed line to a water cache they'd left on top.

The next day was as they'd expected—long hours and hard work in the heat. They climbed the last two pitches in the dark, then looked around for the fixed line. When they couldn't find it, they realized that their only course of action was to bivouac again and locate the rope in the daylight.

They'd been rationing water all day and finished it on the last pitch; Robert was particularly dehydrated—his arms were cramping and he felt sick. It was a dry, unpleasant bivouac and so windy in the notch that night that they got little sleep.

The next morning they spotted their rope peeking over a ledge 150 feet or more above them. There was no way they could retrieve it, and they knew that their easy exit was gone. They could see a possible climbing route out of the notch, but they'd heard it was difficult and poorly protected. Good free climbers under normal conditions, they were so physically and psychologically drained that no one felt it was worth the risk.

The next option was to go down. A bolted rappel route descends steep slabs just east of the Direct Route. However, they had not brought an emergency bolt kit, so there would be no escape if just one anchor turned out to be damaged. The logical choice was to rappel the route they'd climbed, but they felt too exhausted to spend at least one more day in the sun, without water, reversing all 13 pitches.

Their perch gave them a clear view of Yosemite Village, 2500 feet directly below, and when they recognized the vehicle of a friend pulling up to the NPS SAR Office, it was an easy decision to start yelling and waving their portaledge fly. With the help of a loudspeaker and telescope, the NPS figured out the problem and sent a team to hike to the rim, rappel partway, and throw the hung up rope down to the stranded party.

Analysis

When one of the rescuers rappelled to free the fixed line, he found it neatly piled on a ledge 100 feet below its anchor, out of view of the rim because of the rounded nature of the face. Either a hiker had come along and pulled up the rope out of curiosity (or maliciousness?), or it had piled up there when Art first threw it over. He hadn't brought a harness that day, so he couldn't rappel to check the placement directly. From his viewpoint, he had been pretty sure he'd seen the end of the rope at the bottom, but now he'll never know for sure. Furthermore, he now realizes the importance of anchoring the bottom of the line as well as the top.

Here are two more reasons to go down the entire line: First, to locate any sharp edges and protect the rope against them. Second, to anchor the rope in one or more intermediate spots. This minimizes the amount of time the rope is abrading on an edge as a climber ascends, and allows more than one person to ascend simultaneously.

Art, Robert, and Eric agreed that if they'd brought more water they would have been willing to rappel, or even to tackle the climb out. Based on a minimum requirement of two liters per day, plus a day or more of reserve, they were short before they started. They pointed out, themselves, that they didn't carefully do the math, but just looked at the pile of bottles and figured it was enough. In other words, pay as much attention to your water as you do to your rack.

Finally, being able to yell to your friends is a classic benefit of Valley climbing. In a more remote part of the park, such as Mt. Watkins, Art, Robert, and Eric may have been forced to solve the problem on their own. (Source: John Dill, NPS Ranger, Yosemite National Park)

(Editor's Note: Other reports from California included a description of a fall on hard snow in the Sierra Nevada in October and twelve incident summaries from Joshua Tree National Park.

The fall on North Palisades was serious, involving multiple fractures and lacerations, and a difficult evacuation. John Miksits, who sent forward the details, pointed out many lessons learned, mostly from the resulting long evacuation and remoteness of the accident scene. These included having adequate clothing and a stove, knowing first aid, having the phone numbers and addresses of everyone in your party, and having spare batteries for headlamps.

Of the twelve Joshua Tree incidents reported, eight were considered to be non-climbing, involving hikers who were boulder hopping, scrambling, and being overdue. Of the three climbing incidents, one was a fatality and the other two were solo climbers who took serious falls. The reports received focused on the rescues. There were very few details on the accidents themselves.)

FALL ON ROCK, PROTECTION PULLED OUT, NO HARD HAT
Colorado, Rocky Mountain National Park, The Book

On February 6 at 1600, Kevin Hare (19) was leading the 5.9 traverse pitch near the top of J Crack (III, 5.9) on The Book formation. One of Hare's feet slipped on the face climbing section of the traverse pitch. He suffered a lead fall, swinging left, back beneath the last piece of protection he had placed in the hand crack at the start of the traverse. The piece pulled out, and Hare fell 30–40 feet onto a ledge, landing on his stomach. He sustained a fractured finger, laceration to the back of his head, and bruising to his lower back. Hare's belayer, Katelyn Shumaker, was able to lower him to the base of the route to await park rescue personnel.

Analysis

The traverse out of the J Crack is difficult and complicated by some tough route finding. One really needs to be more than just a 5.9 leader to negotiate this pitch. Because the face traverse section is completely unprotected, the final placement in the hand crack needs to be bombproof. The prudent leader may use an extra piece as part of that anchor to insure the integrity of the anchor. Because Mr. Hare was not wearing a hard hat, he sustained a head injury. (Source: Jim Detterline, Longs Peak Ranger)

RAPPEL ERROR – SLACK IN ROPE, FALL ON ROCK
Colorado, Rocky Mountain National Park, Twin Owls

On June 25 Todd Burke had led the first pitch of Organ Pipes (II, 5.6) on the Twin Owls formation. He then pulled the rope up through all pieces of protection and threw one end of the rope down to Claudine Perrault (29). The plan was for Perrault to attach their packs to the rope so that Burke could pull them up rather than return to the base to get them or carry them up the route. However, when Burke tossed the rope, it snagged, leaving the lower end 20–30 feet above the ground. Perrault climbed unroped to the rope end and pulled on it, causing a length of slack to come free and the rope end to fall to the ground. Perrault then attempted to rappel, assuming that the slack was out of the rope. But it was not. She fell 30 feet, sustaining a concussion and minor spinal injuries.

Analysis

The accident itself is the immediate result of failure by both Burke and Perrault to test the rappel adequately by pulling slack out from both ends. However, the underlying and ultimate cause of the accident is the faulty tactical planning by the leader. Acceptable alternatives to the tactics include 1) climb while wearing packs; 2) take just bare necessities; 3) take an extra rope, light weight 7–9 mm, as a haul line; and/or 4) take the extra time to return to the base of the route to pick up non-essential equipment left in packs. (Source: Jim Detterline, Longs Peak Ranger)

FALL ON ROCK, INADEQUATE BELAY
Colorado, Rocky Mountain National Park, The Book

On June 28 at 1015, Dale Yang (31) fell while leading the first pitch of the J

Crack (III, 5.9) on The Book formation. Yang's belayer, Lance Polonbo, released the belay to brace himself for the fall. Polonbo then unsuccessfully attempted to re-grab the rope, but Yang's fall was instead stopped by a ledge. The 30-foot fall resulted in lower back injuries and a rescue for Yang.

Analysis

Many belay devices will automatically lock if the belayer is knocked unconscious or inattentive for other reasons. The Gri-Gri is an example of one such auto locking belay device. Two key factors to remember here: The belayer must not let go with the brake hand and should be tied in to an anchor system—even if on the ground. Belaying is a skill that should be practiced and perfected in a controlled environment. (Source: Jim Detterline, Longs Peak Ranger)

FALL ON ROCK, FAILED TO FOLLOW ROUTE, INADEQUATE PROTECTION, NO HARD HAT
Colorado, Rocky Mountain National Park, Hallett Peak

On July 28, Frederick Sperry (28) was attempting to lead the second pitch of the Culp Bossier Route (III, 5.8) on Hallett Peak. Sperry should have followed the crack starting off the left side of the ledge, but instead he started off route from the center of the ledge and through a small roof to an unprotected face. Sperry realized his error, but instead of down-climbing, he attempted to traverse right toward the crack on the Jackson Johnson Route. After traversing approximately 30 feet with no protection, Sperry slipped and fell 70–80 feet, including a substantial pendulum. Sperry said that as he fell he scraped his back, hurt both ankles, broke a finger, and struck his head on a ledge, causing a three-inch laceration.

Analysis

Routes on the North Face of Hallett Peak are notorious for route finding difficulties. To increase chances of success with route finding, study the guidebook carefully and frequently, and look up, right, left and all around to consider and plan all options. Don't force the route to fit the description, however. If the path chosen doesn't feel right, back off before retreat becomes impossible. Then reevaluate route options, including total retreat. As for a hard hat, Mr. Sperry, like Mr. Hare on The Book (above), sustained a head injury because he was not wearing one. (Source: Jim Detterline, Longs Peak Ranger)

FALLING ROCK – DISLODGED BY CLIMBER, FAILURE TO TEST HOLDS
Colorado, Rocky Mountain National Park, Little Twin Owls

On August 7 at 1900, Bryan Pollack (36) was ascending the Descent Route (I, 5.2) on Little Twin Owls formation to place a top rope set up on the Finger Crack. Approximately ten feet above a ledge, Pollack pulled out a block of rock weighing about 40 pounds. Pollack stepped down to the ledge, but the rock struck him in the left leg, crushing it against another rock. Pollack sustained a fractured left femur and injuries to his knee and lower leg. He was able to move himself to a position of comfort atop a rock fin while his partner went to get park rescue assistance.

Analysis

The descent route on Little Twin Owls is both ascended and descended by countless numbers of climbers every year and is as clean and solid as any route gets. This accident emphasizes the need to test holds as a matter of routine procedure before weighting them, even though it doesn't guarantee that you won't dislodge a loose rock. Mr. Pollack is to be commended for executing the evasive maneuver back to the ledge that probably saved his life, although it is unfortunate that he still sustained serious injuries.

Questions may be raised regarding the appropriateness of climbing unroped on this easy route. The answers are not so definitive. A rope may have allowed Mr. Pollack to jump safely away, but possibly it would also have kept him in the direct line of the falling rock, allowed for leader fall injuries, allowed for the rope to be struck and broken, and/or potentially have placed a belayer in grave danger. (Source: Jim Detterline, Longs Peak Ranger)

EXHAUSTION – UNABLE TO DESCEND, DEHYDRATION, EXCEEDING ABILITIES
Colorado, Rocky Mountain National Park, Longs Peak

On September 1, a Colorado Mountain School guide reported to park rangers that Tim Ashwood (40), a climber with cerebral palsy who had been on the Diamond of Longs Peak for eight days, was ill and would need assistance in descending on the following morning. Ashwood was assisted by partners Jim Thurman and Matt Bliss in jumarring up the Diamond. Park rangers responded on September 2 with a horse to evacuate Ashwood to Longs Peak Trailhead, where he was transported by ambulance to Estes Park Medical Center. Ashwood was suffering from low energy levels, nausea, and dehydration. He was treated with four liters of IV fluid.

Analysis

While Ashwood is to be commended for his perseverance in attempting the realization of his dream—a climb of the Diamond—the nature of his condition and the inability of Ashwood and his partners to manage his energy levels and hydration were the primary causes of this incident. Contributory causes discovered by investigating park rangers included an obsessive desire of Ashwood in wanting to complete this climb at any cost. He had already failed several times. Also, there was commercial interest on the part of Ashwood's partners, amateur guides intending to profit from the publicity they got for hosting the climb. (Source: Jim Detterline, Longs Peak Ranger)

FALL ON ICE, INADEQUATE PROTECTION, POOR TOOL PLACEMENT, EXCEEDING ABILITIES
Colorado, Rocky Mountain National Park, Hidden Falls

On December 20, Ben Johnson (21) was leading Hidden Falls Left (I, WI, 3+) belayed by Krys Obrzut. Johnson climbed the first steep step to the ledge and placed the only screw he used on the route. Johnson continued up the vertical face and was climbing confidently and aggressively. He was attempting to make the transition from the vertical to the belay ledge when his accident occurred. Johnson had one and possibly both hand tools placed on an upward facing edge/ flake of ice about 1.5 feet long by two inches thick. As he stepped high with his left foot, the weight transferred to the hand tools broke the ice flake. Johnson tumbled backward and upside down, striking the ledge with his right shoulder, which took most of the force, and then struck his head. Johnson then flew over the first step but came to rest four to five feet from hitting the ground, finally caught up by his ice screw and belayer. The total length of the fall was 60 feet. Johnson sustained a fractured scapula, collapsed lung, and minor head injuries.

Analysis

Contributing factors in this fall include poor hand tool placements, relying with too many points on a thin and water-weakened ice feature (the flake), overly aggressive climbing style and attitude, inexperience, insufficient protection (only one screw) and nothing to prevent an impact fall to the ledge. The ice flake may have been weakened by water flowing from above in greater than normal amounts due to an illegal ditching operation by a local climber.

Johnson was wearing a Petzl Rockhelmet, which may be credited with minimizing his head injuries. He was knocked unconscious, sustained a forehead laceration from hitting the sharp edge of the helmet, and went into convulsions, but he did not suffer a concussion. (Source: Jim Detterline, Longs Peak Ranger) *(Editor's Note: There were no accidents in Eldorado Canyon this year. However, I received several brief reports on incidents in Boulder Canyon, Flatirons, and Mt. Sanitas, forwarded by Bill May. These mostly involved bouldering. Attention was also called to the avalanche fatalities involving hikers. One lengthy—6,000 word—report gleaned from the internet and entitled "Death and Transfiguration" told of a serious fall due to inadequate protection (belayer and rappel anchors) on Green Mountain Pinnacle. The website is www.geocites.com)*

VARIOUS FALLS ON ROCK, PROTECTION PULLED OUT, ROCK FLAKE (HANDHOLD) CAME OUT, STRANDED
Idaho, City of Rocks National Reserve, Various Routes

There were six climbing incidents reported from this area. Five involved falls from routes, and in three of those, protection came out. In one case, the climber couldn't clip in to a bolt hanger. One climber became stranded while he was free soloing due to a sudden storm. The average age for the victims was late twenties, all experienced.

Analysis

We had no reported climbing accidents in 1997 and only one in 1998. Due to the nature of climbing at the City of Rocks—long response times by ambulance and close proximity to vehicles—there are undoubtedly many climbing accidents that go unreported.

A refreshing trend here is that folks seem to have stopped dropping each other! We haven't had a belay failure for several years. What we have seen however is an increase in protection failure on traditional climbs. My guess is that this is due, at least in part, to renewed interest in clean climbing as the pendulum swings away from sport climbing. These folks are finding out the hard way that protection is only as good as one's ability to place it! Of the six incidents enclosed, three were the result of protection failure. On all of the climbs involved, it is quite straightforward for an experienced climber to protect.

Two of the other incidents were the result of the climber falling low on the climb and hitting a bad landing zone without impacting the belay at all. One had not reached the first bolt on a sport climb, the other spaced his protection too far apart.

The last was a simple pick off of a soloist who at least had the sense to stay put after a sudden squall left the rock wet and slippery. (Source: Brad Shilling, Climbing Ranger)

ROCK BROKE OFF, FALL ON ROCK, CLIMBING UNROPED, FAILURE TO TEST HOLDS, INADEQUATE PROTECTION, INEXPERIENCE
Kentucky, Red River Gorge State Park

On October 2, a climber (22) was on top of Courthouse Rock looking for an anchor placement for rappelling. He had his harness on but was unroped. He went near the edge and the rock broke off underneath him, resulting in his fall off the cliff of about 75 feet, with an additional 25 feet of tumbling at the bottom. His partner went to get help, and three hours later, a search and rescue team arrived and brought the victim out on a rolling backboard. He suffered a pneumothorax and fractured arms.

Analysis

Rappelling is a very popular activity in this park. The victim reported that he had limited experience and was unfamiliar with the area. The sandstone in this area is unstable, but there are plenty of trees to anchor to while exploring around the top of the cliff. Many of the accidents here are the result of hikers, etc., getting drunk and falling off. (Source: Jason Maddux, M.D.)

FALLS ON ROCK AND ICE
Maine, Baxter State Park, Mount Katahdin

There were three incidents reported from Mount Katahdin, all of them happening in February. Scant details were provided. Two involved ice climbers injuring their knees, the third a fall from the Cilly Barber route.

There were a total of 41 search and rescue missions in the park for the year. (Source: Irvin Caverly, Jr., Director, Baxter State Park)

FALL OR SLIP ON ROCK, INADEQUATE EQUIPMENT, INADEQUATE PROTECTION, FAILURE TO FOLLOW ROUTE, NO HARD HAT
North Carolina, Looking Glass Rock, The Nose

On June 19, Keith Ballencourt (30) and two less experienced friends were climbing The Nose (5.8), one of the most popular routes on the mountain. PW, a local guide, spoke with Keith, who described himself as an experienced lead climber at Stone Mountain, NC, an area notorious for long run outs and steep friction. According to PW, Keith was carrying a "Yosemite style rack" (a bandolier which was FULL of assorted gear). PW gave Keith route beta and even held in his hand the specific cams that Keith needed to protect the route. PW relates the rest of the incident: "I didn't really watch him climb, as I was instructing beginners at the base of Peregrine (a climb adjacent to the Nose). The time was about 3:00 p.m. I heard the unforgettable and unmistakable sound of someone falling—scraping and bouncing down the mountain! When I looked up, it seemed that he was falling from either Peregrine or the new rappel line or possibly the top of the mountain, as his speed was considerable. I noticed two people at the lower rappel anchor. I was afraid that he was going to hit, or come close to us at the base of Peregrine. When he was approximately 50 feet from the ground, he began being pulled towards The Nose and came to rest with his feet approximately four feet off the ground! He never lost consciousness but was stunned and disoriented. It seems a miracle that his injuries were not more severe, especially since he wasn't wearing a helmet (Keith suffered a fractured right leg and head injury). He was also very fortunate to have such a skilled group of people in the vicinity (a doctor and EMT were in the area, probably the climbers PW noted on the lower rappel anchor).

"I am afraid that (due to his position on the rock) he may have been climbing below and to the right of the ramp in an effort to reach the lower rappel anchor on Peregrine, as I'm sure that he could see the two climbers there. All of this in spite of the fact that I gave him clear directions to climb the white streak/ramp on the Nose."

The rescue squad was on the scene in just under an hour. He was carried out via litter and transported to the Pisgah Center for Wildlife Education (fish hatchery) to a waiting helicopter. He was evacuated to Mission St. Joseph's Hospital in Asheville, NC.

Analysis

Looking Glass offers climbers steep terrain and limited fixed protection, thus requiring climbers to be familiar with placing gear. Stone Mountain (an area familiar to Keith) is not as steep and almost all protection is fixed. Keith may have benefited by having a better knowledge of the route and placing gear. Also consider placing more gear, especially in unfamiliar territory and when the opportunity presents itself. Wearing a helmet is also a good idea. (Source: Bryan Haslam, PW, and *The Asheville Citizen Times*, June 20 and 21)

FALL ON ROCK – RAPPELLED OFF END OF ROPES
North Carolina, Grandfather Mountain, Shiprock

Okie McCornis (28) and his partner spent July 17 climbing on Shiprock, a popular climbing area located on Grandfather Mountain's East Side. After ascending B.O.G. (5.11), both climbers began their descent by rappelling from Boardwalk (5.8), a common rappel point. Both climbers had done this rappel twice during the day. They used a single rope doubled for the descent, making use of the intermediate station approximately 70 feet up the Boardwalk face on its leftmost side.

Prior to descending they heard thunder in the distance and rain was imminent. While on rappel, Okie forgot about using the intermediate rappel point and rappelled off the end of his rope. He landed at the base of Firepoint, luckily missing the large rocks at the base of the cliff. He sustained a broken left humerus, a bruised lung, several cracked lower vertebrae, and several small cuts.

He was packaged in a litter and carried to the Blue Ridge parkway a short distance away. He was transported to medical facilities in Johnson City, TN, via helicopter.

Analysis
It is not known whether the impending thunderstorm may have hastened the descent. Climbers should take precautionary measures when rappelling by utilizing some type of safeguard or "backup." Always tie a knot at the rope end; use a prusik or other backup (kleimheist knot, autoblock, etc); and be familiar with your surroundings. (Source: Randy Franklin)

FALL ON ROCK, EXCEEDING ABILITIES, FAILURE TO FOLLOW ROUTE, NO HARD HAT
North Carolina, Looking Glass Rock, Bloody Crack
In late November, two people began climbing Bloody Crack (5.8), a popular rock climb on the south side of Looking Glass. The first pitch to Stage Ledge was completed without incident. One of the climbers was leading the second pitch when he moved off route (due to wet rock on the face) onto the arete. He had placed four or five pieces of protection in the main crack. However, he was unable to place gear on the arete. He climbed to a point approximately 20 feet above his last piece when he fell. His fall was partially broken by the tree at the base of the pitch. He landed in a crack on Stage Ledge (on his back), suffering numerous lacerations and a concussion. He was not wearing a helmet. The backpack he was wearing absorbed the majority of the impact, sparing him further head injury.

Brevard Rescue Squad and EMS arrived on the scene, stabilized the patient and executed a litter lower. The patient was carried out, assisted by Job Corps personnel, and transported to Transylvania County Hospital.

Analysis
This climber moved off route because of wet rock. With more experience he may have been able to negotiate the wet rock or the new terrain. Wearing a helmet could have minimized head injury. (Source: Bill Zink)

FALLING ROCK – BLOCK PULLED OFF
New Mexico, Sandia Mountain Wilderness, Hail Peak
After breakfast and coffee, Sinjin Eberle and I set out to have a nice day for a multi pitch 5.8 climb of Hail Peak on May 9, Mother's Day. The weather was warm and stable with a storm possibly moving in later that evening. The Sandias typically keep many climbers away because of the long approach times and thick raspberry and oak groves. We got an early start and planned to be off the climb by mid-afternoon with only a moderate pace.

As many climbers in the Sandias can attest, the old granite is great to climb, but the amount of loose rock is a major drawback, especially on approaches to many areas. The primitive approach to Hail Peak is no exception, with a two-hour fourth- and fifth-class terraced traverse that steadily gains exposure as Echo Canyon drops below.

I had just scrambled my way up some loose blocks and saw Sinjin about 40 meters behind so as not to risk getting hit by rock fall. Sinjin asked, "How does it look?"

"O.K., as long as you don't pull on anything too hard," I replied. Then all of a sudden I heard a quiet "Oh... Marc..." I turned to look back and saw that Sinjin had pulled an incredibly large piece of granite loose. He lost his footing on the sandy slope attempting to balance the rock back into position for enough time to escape its path. The boulder expanded from the face and first crushed Sinjin's hands and then rolled on top of him. I tried to tell him to jump (out of the way), but it was clear that I was getting ready to watch a friend die.

All I could see of Sinjin was from the middle of his shins down and the top of his head. The rock covered the rest of his body and was dragging him down the slope I had just crossed. The ledge was only two to three meters wide and ended abruptly with some yuccas and a 50-meter cliff. Somehow, with the inertia of the rock (250–300 kg) and all of his strength, Sinjin was able to get the rock off of himself, but not before it clipped him in the back of the head, throwing him around like a rag doll. Blood was flying in the air from his crushed hands and torn open leg.

I yelled at him not to move as he could have easily rolled once and gone the distance. He managed to hook a foot on a bush and maintain his position, as he was still remarkably responsive. I have seen a lot of trauma from ten plus years of EMS, and I could tell already from the extent of his injuries that he would need a trauma center. Fortunately, I had brought a cell phone. With one hand I was calling a friend from the Mountain Rescue team and with the other I was setting an anchor so I could lower Sinjin off the rock. I called Steve Attaway:

"Steve, how are you?" He knew me right away.

"Good, how are you?"

"Fine, but Sinjin needs a helicopter to the West Face of Hail Peak—he's been crushed by a rock."

"O.K., see ya soon." Steve knew the situation was critical and didn't dally around with details. He knew the right people to call at the New Mexico State Police and he immediately got the rescue team in motion at the same time. The call was short, but it was all that was needed and I had to save my phone battery for later.

Meanwhile I managed to assess Sinjin and see that his hands were crushed, bleeding and useless to him. His leg was split open at the shin but not obviously broken although he could bear little weight and had numbness in his right foot. But perhaps worse was that his arms and neck were severely bruised. Crush syndrome could easily ensue from the mechanism of injury and organ failure was a real possibility. He was also facing the permanent loss of his hands or arms and major lifestyle changes. I did all the medical care I could with a sparse first aid kit and then got him ready for a long lower.

I could not do a standard pick off because the only anchor was questionable at best, and I had to back it up with my own body weight. So, after determining

Sinjin most likely did not have a dangerous spinal injury, it was necessary to lower him off the ledge for a rescue team to gain access to him. Sinjin became courageous enough to be lowered off the cliff and was able to maintain most of his weight on one foot until he reached the bottom. Although he could manage this, he could not walk, and attempting to do so would exacerbate the situation. All fours were needed to get out of the canyon and Sinjin had maybe one and a half at best.

Hours later, Jen Semon and Steve arrived with a rescue medical kit and we gave Sinjin a desperately needed IV and narcotics. Moments after that, a Kirkland Air Force Base CH 53 helicopter arrived with a Para-rescue team. The winds were shifty at about ten to fifteen knots, but the down draft in that little vertical canyon made it seem like a hurricane. Sinjin was lifted by winch at a 35–40-degree angle with a tag line and taken to the hospital. A ground rescue for Sinjin would have been complicated and absolutely taken into the next day. The storm that came in an hour after the rescue had gale forces that would have made it impossible for the CH 53. This would have proven a bad outcome for his medical well-being as he would most likely have lost a major portion of his hands and possibly his foot to secondary infection and sepsis. He spent an extra two hours in surgery to make his hands functional again.

Analysis

What I learned from this experience is that good decision making, being prepared, being lucky, and good, fast connections can all come together to escape disaster. Sometimes a safer route cannot be taken, so it is important to realize when the danger zone is present. It was a humbling experience for both of us to find ourselves at the mercy of nature, especially since we have many years of climbing experience between us. (Source: Marc Beverly)

FALL ON ROCK, CLIMBING ALONE AND UNROPED, INADEQUATE CLOTHING, EXCEEDING ABILITIES
New Mexico, Organ Mountains, Organ Needle

On December 1, John Smith (name changed) was reported overdue from a solo climb of the 4th-class route up the Organ Needle (9,012 feet). Following a lengthy search, his body was found at the base of a 60-foot frozen waterfall on the east side of Dark Canyon, directly below the Organ Needle. The subject had apparently fallen while either attempting an unnamed fifth-class route from below the Dark Canyon Saddle to the summit of the Organ Needle, or traversing below the south side of the summit. He had apparently survived the initial fall but suffered a second fatal fall while attempting to down-climb the ice.

Analysis

Reports from friends and family indicated this man was experienced in this area; however, he was clearly exceeding his abilities. The subject was clothed in cotton jeans and a light cotton jacket. While unusually mild weather existed at low elevations, temperatures at summit elevation were regularly below freezing. The exact details of the accident will never be known, but the subject appeared to be attempting either an unroped solo climb or an unroped traverse. And, while he survived the initial fall, he was apparently disoriented, so in attempting to climb back down the mountain, chose the wrong route. It is unclear whether the subject would have survived the wait for rescue with the head injuries sustained in the initial fall. (Source: Tim Manning, Albuquerque Mountain Rescue)

VARIOUS FALLS ON ROCK, INADEQUATE BELAYS, NO OR INADEQUATE PROTECTION, NO HARD HAT
New York, Mohonk Preserve, Shawangunks
There were 28 climbing-related accidents reported this year. Eighteen involved leader falls, six involved top roping or seconding, and one was a rappel error. There were three bouldering-related accidents that resulted in minor injuries. These were due to poor spotting or missing the landing pad. Bouldering is gaining in popularity again.

Seven falls resulted in fractures, one in a dislocation, and two in concussions, one of which was due to no hard hat. The rest, with the exception of the fatality described below, included bruises and lacerations. Three of the reports indicated poor rope handling, either with too much slack in the rope or not enough rope to lower the climber to the ground. Several mishaps were due to leading grades above the climbers' abilities.

One cliff rescue was performed on the poplar climb "Hawk" (5.4) in the Trapps. The leader had fallen on the second pitch, and the old piton he had clipped into pulled out of the rock. Due to his ankle injury, the climber needed to be lowered from the top of the first pitch by litter. (Source: From the annual report submitted by the Mohonk Preserve and Jed Williamson)

RAPPEL ERROR – WEBBING ANCHOR NOT TIED, FALL ON ROCK
New York, Mohonk Preserve, Shawangunks
On October 14, Scott Ruit (29) fell about 80 feet to his death while attempting to rappel from Birdland. He set up an extended anchor using webbing, weighted it, and the fall began as the webbing came away from the anchor.
Analysis
Ruit's rope was found on the ground with carabiners attached to it. A piece of unsecured nylon webbing was found hanging from the anchor. When Ruit went to weight the rope, it apparently dropped through the 25-foot webbing, which Ruit probably thought was tied. It did not appear that there was anything wrong with the equipment or the fixed protection.

Ruit was described by locals as a good friend and a competent climber who was a cautious, experienced climber and who did not push his limits. (Source: Kirsten Conley, *The Times Herald*, and the Mohonk Preserve annual report)

FALL ON SNOW, WEATHER – UNSTABLE SNOW CONDITIONS, FAULTY USE OF CRAMPONS
Oregon, Mount Hood, Cooper Spur Route
Carey Cardon (31) and his wife Tena Cardon (29) were experienced mountaineers training for a proposed climb of Mt. McKinley. They started climbing the

Cooper Spur at 0430 on May 23. They summited about 0800 via the 2,000-foot, 50-degree snow slope that capped the 4,500-foot route above their tent. On the descent, one of the Cardons slipped just below the summit and they tumbled roped together more than 2,000 feet down the mountain to their deaths.

Analysis

The Cooper Spur Route below the summit of Mt. Hood is notoriously dangerous, having caused the deaths of at least 13 climbers preceding the Cardons. The Oregon Mountaineering Association's route description states, "Particular caution should be taken on descent, and some climbers arrange a shuttle … so that they may descend the standard route." *Oregon High, a Climbing Guide* by Jeff Thomas states, "Do not descend Cooper Spur… during periods of hot weather, as the snow becomes excessively soft…" *The Summit Guide to the Cascade Volcanoes* by Jeff Smoot states, "It is quite steep and exposed. Falls from this route are common and often fatal…"

A spring heat wave and the strong morning sun had dangerously softened the snow on the Cooper Spur Route on this day. Joren Bass and his partner had ascended the route at the same time as the Cardons. Bass decided to descend an alternate, safer route. "We were kind of surprised that they were going back down that way."

An eye witness reported that he was certain that both climbers were wearing crampons. Therefore it is probable that snow was balling up in them. One rescue team member said that Carey Cardon was found with his crampons on, while Tena was not so found. A professional climbing guide named Charles Hsieh rendered this opinion: "There were no gross errors in judgment." However, the facts suggest otherwise. (Sources: Robert Speik, Jed Williamson, and *The Oregonian*, May 25)

FALL ON HARD SNOW, INEXPERIENCE
Oregon, South Cascades, Broken Top

On September 19 in the Three Sisters Wilderness area, Bonnie Lamb (39) was ascending a volcanic talus and scree ridge on Broken Top when she came to a short, steep section of surface-softened hard-snow near the 9,175 south summit. She slipped and rocketed about 300 yards down the slope coming to a stop in the rough scree below. Unconscious for 15 minutes and with a severely injured scalp and nose, she was aided by climber Vince Hudson, a former medic, who described her fall as follows: "Originally she was sliding just flat. Then she went over a rock ledge and started to tumble, head over heels, and started picking up speed. Then she went over another ledge and I could see her head hit it. I couldn't believe how fast she was going. It was just like you throw a Raggedy Ann doll off a cliff. She seemed [to be going] 60 to 70 mph easy."

Analysis

Surface-softened hard-snow slopes have claimed many innocent victims. An ice ax quickly used could have stopped the initial slide. Modern ultralight ice axes are a good companion on spring hikes and climbs. Had somebody not witnessed her fall, she might not have survived. (Source: Robert Speik)

FALLING ROCKS – BROKE AWAY FROM ROUTES
Pennsylvania, Delaware Water Gap National Recreation Area, Mount Minsi, Mount Tammany

There were three climbing incidents reported from this area.

The first report was of a fall on a route called Raptor of the Steep (5.10) on Mount Minsi. Dan O'Malley was about 25 feet above a belay site. His partner Tim Feitzinger watched him make a move to climb up on a large rock. The rock teetered and then came free from the face, knocking O'Malley backward and off the mountain. The rock nearly hit Feitzinger. While he was busy avoiding the rock, he lost track of O'Malley. Then he realized that O'Malley was not on belay because the rock had severed the rope. A third partner, Jeff Sukenick, began efforts to get help for O'Malley, who was seriously injured. Sukenick and Feitzinger, and then two paramedics, were unable to revive O'Malley.

In July on Mount Tammany, Laura Glockeler was ascending a fixed rope when she began to pendulum. She reached for a large rock and it broke off, crushing her left arm in the process. She required reattachment surgery, which was successful.

In August on Mount Minsi, another accident involved a fall to a ledge as a result of a rock (foothold) coming loose. The climber, Dr. Mike Sinclair, fell about 20 feet onto a ledge. His injuries included a pneumothorax, torn cervical ligament, several fractures (T5&6, ribs, hip), lacerations, and a concussion. He survived, thanks to a technical rescue effort involving a dozen people. During the rescue, part of the ledge gave way, and while a rescuer below was trying to run from possible harm, he broke his ankle. (Source: Incident Reports submitted by Delaware Water Gap NRA)

FALLING ICE – UNSTABLE ROUTE, MISJUDGED CONDITIONS
Utah, Sastaquin Canyon

We had a five-day warm spell followed by a weak cold front for 36 hours prior to the climb. Overnight temperatures had been well below freezing, so the ice was brittle.

We climbed the approach pitch to the first ledge. From here we could see the pillar hung mostly free for about 50 feet, almost touching the ground. A week earlier, this route was barely touching the ground and had been climbed. Now there was a crack and four inches of space near the ground showing that the pillar had retracted in response to the weather conditions. Looking at the ice structure caused my partner and me to comment on its apparent instability. She was convinced it was unsafe and suggested that we climb a different route. I had climbed this route in a different year when it was not touching down, though its dimensions looked less stable this day. I climbed up without really swinging my tools, either hooking or tapping my picks in on the bottom overhang, then chimneying between the ice and the rock, once that was possible. There is a bolted line on the rock behind the pillar that is a dry tool variation. I had clipped in to one bolt about 25 feet from the ground. About 40 feet up, I felt like I was past the most unstable part. I was near the place where the ice attached to the rock about ten feet above me. The pillar was about six feet in diameter. The second bolt I wanted to clip in to was not an easy reach, so I swung my pick into the ice with intentions of reaching the bolt by leaning off a secure pick placement. But the placement caused a clean shear across the pillar, propagating instantly from the point of contact. I fell a split second behind the falling pillar due to the friction of my butt against the rock. Right above the ground, I was arrested by the rope, but I was not spared the shower of large ice chunks. I ended up with broken ribs and shoulder and a deeply bruised leg. My wife was belaying 50 feet to the side, tied to a tree. It took us about three hours to get to the car, usually a half hour jaunt.

Analysis

The warming trend had probably created a lot of tension in the ice underneath its point of attachment. The cold night had made the ice brittle, so long, running fractures were more likely. The danger was fairly obvious. The lapse was in my perception of my ability to deal with the danger. I was too focused on doing this particular route. Also, I was complacent because I had climbed many similar structures with no mishap.

In hindsight, I can see I was lucky to get away with relatively minor injuries. My choice to climb an unstable route endangered the follower, since she could have caused the entire structure to collapse near the bottom, which would be almost certain death. (Source: Seth Shaw)

FALLING ROCK, FAILURE TO TEST HOLDS, LEADER'S LAPSE LEAD TO MISJUDGMENT
Utah, Uinta Mountains – Between Gunsight Pass and Kings Peak

On June 29, Lucy (42), a beginning climber, was climbing above the leader (71) on an ascent near Kings Peak. She tried to stand on a precarious cluster of rocks and managed to dislodge four of them, varying in weight from an estimated 50 to 1,400 pounds. This resulted in a fractured ankle, multiple abrasions and lacerations, and a sprained knee.

Her leg was pinned under one rock, which had to be levered off. The ensuing rescue was complicated by the victim's husband being in psychogenic shock and giving the wrong location of the accident to rangers via phone.

Analysis

Being slower at age 71 and on a remarkably stable slope, I allowed a novice climber to climb above me. Always enforce discipline with inexperienced members of climbing group. Never allow novices to lead unless closely controlled for training, even if terrain is apparently ultra easy. Anticipate surprise obstacles. (Source: Stan Sattelberg)

FALL ON ROCK, INADEQUATE PROTECTION, PROTECTION PULLED, FATIGUE, WEATHER, INEXPERIENCE
Vermont, Nichol's Ledge

On October 22, Ian (22) and Ryan (23) were attempting to climb the first pitch of a two-pitch route unfamiliar to both. Ian was leading and Ryan was belaying. The weather that day was cloudy, cool (40s), and windy. The first pitch of the climb appeared to be a short 40-foot section that ended at a small tree ledge. The terrain at the base of the climb consisted of steep talus and woods. Ian began climbing the first pitch, placing a #1 Camelot at a point 15 feet above the slope and a second piece at approximately 30 feet up the route. Immediately above the second anchor point, Ian encountered a steep friction slab with a few small edges that lead to the tree ledge above. After making two difficult moves approximately six feet above his last piece of protection (a single HB cam set in a horizontal crack), Ian came to what appeared to be a "dead end" in the route. Ian decided that he would not be able to reverse his moves back down the climb and had no choice but to continue the last few moves to the tree ledge as it was only a few feet away. While attempting a strenuous move, Ian fell. The force of the fall pulled his last piece of protection from the horizontal crack and pitched him feet first toward the ground. Realizing that Ian was going to hit the ground, Ryan stepped forward in an attempt to break his fall. Ian landed on Ryan, and both tumbled down the talus slope becoming tangled in the rope. Their tumble down the slope came to an abrupt stop when the rope pulled tight against the #1 Camelot still anchored in the rock.

Almost immediately after they stopped tumbling, Ryan told Ian not to move and began untangling them from the rope. After checking himself for any injuries (none were found), Ryan began checking Ian for injuries. Both were trained Wilderness First Responders. Ian complained of pain in his right shoulder. Closer examination found that it was dislocated. Ryan attempted to reduce the dislocation in the field, but to no avail. Ryan gathered all the gear and assisted Ian back to their truck. What had been a 15-minute approach to the base of the climb earlier in the day turned into a difficult two-hour retreat. Ryan drove Ian to the hospital in St. Johnsbury, where Ian's dislocation was treated. He was subsequently released that evening.

Analysis

The difficulty of the first pitch was estimated by both climbers to be 5.5. While the route to the tree ledge was obvious, the end of the first pitch presented some climbing difficulties that may have been beyond the climbing ability of the leader. Often overlooked in climbing is the ability of the lead climber to reverse moves when coming to a "dead end." This was Ian's first year of lead climbing. He had done fifteen easy leads prior to this attempt. Ryan had less leading experience.

Both climbers speculate that while climbing above the last anchor point, the cam must have "walked," affecting the orientation of the cams and ultimately the holding power of the device. In hindsight, the leader admitted that he should have placed more than one piece of gear at the last possible anchoring point before attempting to make the last few moves to the tree ledge. In addition, both climbers surmised that fatigue and the cold temperatures contributed to Ian's inability to make the last two difficult moves to the security of the tree ledge.

Finally, it is interesting to note that the first piece of protection placed on the climb ended up being the stop gap that prevented both climbers from tumbling further down the talus slope than they did. Both climbers agreed that had this piece of protection not held the injuries sustained could have been more serious. More importantly, an effective self rescue may not have been possible in this relatively obscure climbing area. (Source: John Kascenska)

FALL ON ICE, CLIMBING ALONE AND UNROPED
Washington, Mount Rainier, Gibraltar Ledge

On March 21, E. Dawes Eddy (56) fell 1600 feet while soloing the Gibraltar Ledge route on Mount Rainier. A four-person climbing team on the same route witnessed the accident and subsequent tumble down the 40–50-degree icy Gibraltar Chute. Eddy's fall was arrested where the slope angle decreased onto the Nisqually Glacier. One member of the witnessing party used a cell phone to alert the National Park Service while another member down-climbed to Eddy.

During the fall, Eddy had sustained bone fractures to his lower right leg and possible internal injuries. That climber helped stabilize Eddy and stayed with him while the other members of his team returned to Camp Muir to retrieve a rescue liter. The Park Service dispatched a helicopter with rangers Brenchley, Turner, and Winslow. They were flown near the accident site where they climbed to Eddy with rescue gear, litter, and medical supplies. Eddy was prepared for extrication and lowered to the helicopter, then flown to a hospital.

Analysis

Eddy had extensive experience climbing Mount Rainier, both solo and in the winter, and therefore understood the risk of his undertaking. Solo climbers in the winter can expect hidden crevasses, poor weather, and, most notably, no backup. Eddy was fortunate that another team was on the same route and witnessed the fall. He stated that no particular event caused the slip to occur, only that he recalled losing his footing and quickly falling backwards, sliding out of control before he could get into a self arrest position. Note that the slope angle was steep—50-degrees, and the snow was hard and icy. There had also been a significant amount of snowfall that winter. This coated the normally rock exposed gully, and he felt the snow helped to cushion his tumbles and prevent more serious injuries. Eddy was wearing his helmet and attributed his survival to this fact. (Source: Mike Gauthier, SAR Ranger, Mount Ranier National Park)

FALL INTO CREVASSE, CLIMBING UNROPED, WEATHER
Washington, Mount Rainier, Muir Snowfield Paradise Glacier

On April 1, Michael Corroone (51) and Dan Gallagher (36) set out to climb Mount Rainier. Severe weather prevented a summit attempt, and they began descending back to Paradise on April 12. High winds, low visibility and white-out conditions continued, forcing them to follow compass bearings down the Muir Snowfield. Near 8,800 feet, the unroped pair simultaneously fell into a deceptively covered crevasse on the Paradise Glacier, the eastern edge of the Muir Snowfield. Gallagher's backpack caught on the slender entrance and he was able to extricate himself. Corroone, however, slipped through the crack and disappeared into the crevasse.

Gallagher set up a snow anchor and lowered a rope to Corroone. However, Corroone was wedged in such a way that he could do little to assist himself or tie off on the rope. Gallagher then resorted to his cell phone and called 911, reaching an operator in Oregon after waiting for some time for cell service coverage. The call was transferred to the Mount Rainier communications center and a rescue was initiated.

Rangers Gauthier and Mallard, while patrolling at Camp Schurman, were notified of the accident and reported that the weather was improving on the upper mountain. A helicopter dispatched from Seattle transported the rescuers from Camp Schurman to the 9,200-foot level on the Muir Snowfield above the accident site. They descended to the crevasse where Gallagher was awaiting assistance. Gallagher reported that his partner had been trapped in the crevasse for over two hours and there had been no communication between them for the last hour and a half. New rescue anchors and rope were quickly put in service and Gauthier hastily rappelled into the crevasse to assess the situation. Eighty feet below, he found Corroone alive but very hypothermic and tightly wedged between the icy walls of the crevasse. He was suspended from his armpits by his backpack straps like a parachutist trapped in a tree. Corroone was unable to feel or use his arms and could do little more than press his legs against the crevasse walls to prevent slipping further.

For over an hour Gauthier dangled, working at times upside down to dislodge Corroone from his trapped position. Once Corroone was freed from his pack and snowshoes, he was pulled onto a small ledge and stabilized in a harness. Mallard and Gallagher then hoisted him to the surface with a Z pulley system.

As the weather seemed to be improving, the helicopter returned to fly Corroone off the mountain. Shortly after it reinserted, a cloud enveloped the landing zone and super-cooled rime ice quickly coated the rotors and turbine intakes of the ship. The helicopter could no longer achieve lift and became grounded. Pilot Uttecht stated, "I don't want to, but I have shut down." Limited daylight and bivouac resources increased the urgency of the new situation. Ice was scraped from the rotors and turbine intakes of the helicopter with snow pickets. After 30 minutes of ice removal, the clouds again cleared and Uttecht decided to try a flight with only Corroone on board. Conditions continued to improve and Corroone was safely lifted off the mountain before sunset. Uttecht then flew subsequent missions to retrieve Gallagher, the rescue gear, Gauthier, and Mallard.

Analysis

Corroone and Gallagher made the right decision to use a compass for navigation when descending under such adverse weather conditions. Traveling unroped is also a common practice on the snowfield. What caused them difficulty was the blowing wind and snow. Despite following the correct compass bearing, strong winds easily blew the team off course. It is like a small airplane flying on bearing with a strong crosswind that will slowly cause it to be blown off route, even though the bearing remains the same. This is what happened to

Corroone and Gallagher. The crevasse fall occurred roughly 100 yards from the main route taken by thousands of climbers in the summer.

Although Gallagher did a good job setting up snow anchors and lowering a rope, this accident demonstrates that more may be necessary to rescue your partner from a crevasse. Climbers who have fallen in a crevasse cannot always help themselves, and teams should always take this into consideration. If the partner falls, can the second member set up the anchors AND rappel into a foreboding crevasse to render assistance? Many teams elect to go with a minimum of three members (four in the winter) to alleviate some of this stress. Climbers turned rescuers need to be mentally prepared for this daunting task.

The pair was fortunate on many counts. One, that they both didn't fall all the way into the crevasse; two, that their cell phone worked (they don't always on Rainier), and three, that two rescuers happened to be on the mountain during the very early season.

Although it was clear when the helicopter landed, the landing zone did not remain as such after a few minutes of waiting. Weather conditions seemed to be improving. However a rogue cloud made the rescue much more interesting and stressful. It was also fortunate that the helicopter did not require more de-icing in harder to access places. Additionally, if the weather had not cleared, it would have been a long night for the pilot with only a flight suit and leather jacket, not to mention Corroone in his severely hypothermic condition.

Corrone, who is married with two teenage daughters and who has climbed for 22 years, said the accident raised his safety standards. "I'm thinking now I wouldn't go out with less than four guys and full battle gear. I made every possible mistake, and I could have paid dearly for this one." (Source: Mike Gauthier, SAR Ranger, Mount Ranier National Park and *The News Tribune*, April 14)

PARTY SEPARATED – ILLNESS, POOR PLANNING AND LOGISTICS, MISCOMMUNICATION
Washington, Mount Rainier, Muir Snowfield Paradise Glacier
John Repka was last seen alive descending the Muir Snowfield on May 16 during a planned day climb with the group One Step At a Time (OSAT). Repka fell behind the main group because he was feeling ill, vomiting and moving slowly. Near 9,000 feet, he turned around with other group members on their descent from Camp Muir. Repka followed the team but could not keep up. Near 8,000 feet in a whiteout, a member of the group warned Repka that he was heading too far west and possibly off route. That group continued to descend believing Repka was either behind them, or that he would be met by another part of the team still descending from Muir.

When the team regrouped in the parking lot and Repka had not arrived, they began communication with him over a two-way radio (which some members were using). Repka radioed that he was near Panorama Point, but he wasn't certain. They lost contact with him after 5:30 p.m. In that conversation, Repka stated that he didn't know his location. A climbing ranger and a volunteer were notified at Camp Muir, and they descended the snowfield attempting to locate him that night. They ran into zero visibility and eventually had to give up.

Teams composed of rangers, mountain rescue volunteers, guides and friends of John Repka searched intensely for the following eight days. Poor visibility, heavy precipitation, high winds, and hazardous terrain hampered their work. Helicopters and air scent dogs greatly aided search efforts during two days of clear weather. The primary search area was thoroughly covered, although a significant amount of new snow fell during the week. The active search was called off on day nine after no clues were found. Rangers remained on alert for potentially emerging clues as the snow melted throughout the summer.

In September during a routine maintenance helicopter flight, pilot Jess Hagerman spotted a body matching the clothing description of Repka in an icefall. It was located near 8,100 feet on the Paradise Glacier (very near where Corroone had fallen). Climbing rangers were flown to the site where they descended to the body and confirmed the observation. Repka was found in his bivy sac next to his ice ax, backpack and two way radio. He had died from exposure, not traumatic injuries, and his remains were flown off the mountain.

Analysis

If one thing can be learned from this accident, it is to stay together and communicate when in teams, especially large ones where organization and management are problematic. Repka was part of a 50-plus person group that day. Somehow though, misunderstandings and assumptions led to his being left behind. The radio also provided a false security. Radios, cell phones, and other electronic devices are not substitutes for critical communication, navigation, and survival needs. (Source: Mike Gauthier, SAR Ranger, Mount Ranier National Park)

FALL ON ROCK, INADEQUATE BELAY, MISCOMMUNICATION
Washington, Peshastin Pinnacles

While I have no memory of this accident, I have been able to reconstruct the event based upon the observations of my climbing partner, Lynn. On May 22, she and I climbed the Tunnel Route (5.6) on Orchard Rock at Peshastin Pinnacles in eastern Washington. Upon reaching the top, I tied into two bolts placed about 15 feet from the vertical edge on a 20-degree slope. Due to the distance of the bolts from the edge, I chose to tie into a long runner (a 20-ft. cordelette tied in half) to be closer for communication while belaying. About 20 ft. from the summit, Lynn was unable to reach a camming unit I had placed in a crack about 4 ft. from the route. She was able to unclip the climbing rope from the sling and proceed to the top. After a brief discussion, we decided to lower her back to the piece, giving her greater access to remove it, while allowing her to climb the most enjoyable part of the route once more.

After making the decision to lower, I turned away from Lynn for some unknown reason while she was standing, still on belay. She thought it was safe to lower and stepped back to weight the rope. Due to miscommunication between us, however, I was not ready for the weight shift, and it pulled me off my feet, swinging me violently around on the long tie in. I slammed the rock with the back of my head, my skull was fractured, and I fell unconscious, losing the belay. Lynn began to fall over the edge of the rappel route and dropped approximately 80 feet to the ground. Her left ankle and right wrist were shattered and her left femur was snapped. Miraculously, she sustained no internal injuries, her femoral artery remained intact, and she had no severe head injuries, as she had chosen not to wear a helmet. She is very, very lucky not to have needed it this time and to have survived a fall severe enough to have killed most people. She remembers seeing and hearing my head hit the rock with such intense force that she firmly believes I would not have survived the impact without the protection of my helmet. Two climbers discovered us roughly ten minutes after the accident, called 911, and began first aid. Chelan County Mountain Rescue arrived with the paramedics and, after a brief description of events from Lynn, began climbing the route to where I was. Meanwhile, as Lynn was being carried to the ambulance, I became conscious and attempted to untie myself from the anchor—a common problem when head injuries have occurred while climbing. Luckily the SAR team was able to convince me to remain anchored until they were able to reach my location to rig a litter for lowering.

I required brain surgery to remove the blood clots that formed after the accident and remained in a coma for 5 days. After that, I was unaware of my identity or where I was for about another week. My memory continued to return slowly over the next several weeks, although I still remember nothing of the accident or anything between May 22 and June 2. I was able to leave the hospital on June 17, but still experienced bouts of severe dizziness and was unable to drive until August. Lynn initially underwent six and one half hours of surgery to repair her injuries, and has required several more surgeries to assist in her recovery. She continues daily rehabilitation.

Analysis

We believe the accident was caused by the instability of the long tie in, miscommunication between us, and my failure to remain in proper position while Lynn was on belay. I should have been sitting, and never should have turned away from my partner. Also, had Lynn clipped into the anchor the moment she reached the top of the pitch, much of this accident could have been prevented. Any one of these factors alone might not have caused any damage; added together, they were catastrophic.

We would both like to thank the two women who found us, called for help, administered first aid, and stayed until the professional rescuers arrived. We would also like to express our deep gratitude to the Chelan County Sheriff, Chelan Mountain Rescue volunteers, and all the doctors, nurses, therapists and friends in Wenatchee and Seattle who assisted in our rescue and helped us begin to recover from this terrible event. The accident deeply affected our families, and is estimated to have created more than $150,000 in rescue and medical expenses. (Source: Greg Sullivan)

FALL ON STEEP ICE WHILE SKIING
Washington, Mount Rainier, Liberty Ridge

A climber at Thumb Rock high camp on the Liberty Ridge called Mount Rainier National Park with a cell phone on the evening of May 24 to report that his climbing partner was missing after a skiing accident en route. David Perrson (31) was telemarking Liberty Ridge from the top when he lost an edge and cart-wheeled out of control, disappearing down the Willis Wall. Perrson fell from the 12,500-foot level near the Black Pyramid, a 50–60-degree icy section of the route.

Rangers Brenchley and Gauthier flew reconnaissance the next morning and identified a body at the 9,800-foot level on the Carbon Glacier. The body lay in the avalanche debris cone of *Thermogensis*, a climbing route notorious for ice and rock avalanches. Shortly after they spotted Perrson, a tremendous avalanche of ice ran the route and partially covered the body. Recovery operations were postponed due to the increasing daytime temperatures and obvious objective hazards. Plans were then drawn for a predawn recovery next morning before the sun warmed the ice cliffs above.

At sunrise on May 26, pilot Hagerman inserted Rangers Gauthier and Olson near the accident. No sign of Perrson could be found. Pilot Uttecht flew avalanche reconnaissance while Rangers Gottlieb and Patterson provided safety and support for the recovery team. An hour of search was needed to locate the body. It had been pushed a substantial distance down slope and reburied by successive avalanches the previous day. There was no chance that Perrson survived the fall and moved under his own power. The body was retrieved without incident and flown off the mountain.

Analysis

David Perrson was an accomplished climber and athlete. He soloed Liberty Ridge the day before just after reaching high camp, then telemarked back down it that evening. Perrson clearly understood the level of commitment and risk involved in such extreme adventures and sadly paid the price for his passion. (Source: Mike Gauthier, SAR Ranger, Mount Ranier National Park)

DROPPED GEAR, INADEQUATE FUEL AND FOOD, WEATHER, DEHYDRATION, EXHAUSTION
Washington, Mount Rainier, Liberty Ridge

A cell phone call late June 30 revealed that Mike Matelich and Larry Sverdrup were stranded on Liberty Ridge and in need of assistance after dropping one of their packs. The pack was lost while breaking camp from an unplanned bivouac above Thumb Rock. Unfortunately, the pack contained their ice screws, which the team felt were necessary to safely complete the route. Complicating matters, one member was having crampon troubles and the weather was deteriorating. Another forced bivy in a crevasse and a few broken cell phone calls later expressing their concern initiated a rescue.

A helicopter was dispatched that evening and inserted teams of rangers at the base of Liberty Ridge and Camp Schurman. A cloud cap prevented flights above 10,000 feet. It was hoped that one of the teams would climb the mountain and meet the stranded climbers on route, assisting them off the mountain. Whiteouts and high winds, however, thwarted rescue plans that night.

The weather the next day had cleared sufficiently allowing a US Army Reserve helicopter to land near the summit with an eight person rescue team. Climbing ranger Olson, Mountain Rescue volunteer Ellsworth and Rainier Mountaineering guides Rausch and T. Richards down-climbed the 55-degree slope beneath Liberty Cap to meet Matelich and Sverdrup. Rausch and T. Richards met the stationary team at 2:00 p.m. near 13,600 feet. Matelich and Sverdrup began climbing again that morning after receiving three ice screws from another passing team. They were, however, seriously dehydrated and exhausted, and their progress was extremely slow. With the assistance of the rescuers, the pair climbed the remainder of the route and were flown off the summit that evening.

Analysis
Matelich and Sverdrup were having a string of bad luck. Inattention to securing gear and a few broken and desperate sounding cell phone calls later led to a rescue. The team commented that they wished they had slept on it "before calling for a rescue... Cell phones make it all too easy to bail..." They also wished that they had brought more fuel with them to melt water. A few days in a snow cave without water also made self help much more difficult.

Liberty Ridge combined with bad weather pins down teams nearly every year on Mount Rainier. But on a similar yet more inspiring note, two climbers, off duty NOLS instructors, were ascending the Liberty Ridge route in May when they overcame another two-person team on the Carbon Glacier. The seasoned NOLS team noted that the slower moving climbers did not assist with trail breaking and also requested belays once on route. Despite the faster team's urge to quickly finish the climb and get off the mountain, they instead elected to ascend with the pair assisting them along the way. Unfortunately the weather deteriorated significantly and what ensued were seven days of rationed survival in snow caves on the upper Liberty Ridge, summit and Disappointment Cleaver. The foursome combined resources and presevered, so perhaps a more tragic accident was prevented by such generosity. (Source: Mike Gauthier, SAR Ranger, Mount Ranier National Park)

LOOSE ROCK CAME OFF – FAILURE TO TEST HOLDS
Washington, North Cascades National Park, Sahale Peak
On June 19, a party of Everett Mountaineers selected a non-standard route up the West Face of Sahale Peak. They were within 50 feet of the 8000-foot summit ridge around 2030 when one of them grabbed a loose rock. It struck him in the face and caused him to fall 30–40 feet. His left arm became tangled in the rope, which caused a dislocation of his shoulder. He also suffered a black eye, broken teeth, and many bruises. Fortunately, he was wearing a helmet.

They were able to return to their camp, where the victim was then transported to the hospital by helicopter. (Source: From a report written by Galen Stark, Ranger at NCNP)

FALL ON ROCK, INADEQUATE PROTECTION, EXCEEDING ABILITIES
Washington, North Cascades, Cutthroat Peak

At 6:00 a.m. on July 17, five climbers started on the South Buttress of Cutthroat Peak. It was clear and warm. The climb started across a snow basin and up steep snow in the highest gully. The group continued up some steep third-class rock to where the gully opened into a notch below the ridge. Dan (34), Annette (32), and Dave (36) were ahead. They roped up and carried gear to the ridge. Todd (38) and Ken (33) left gear and climbed in rock shoes to the ridge from the left of the notch. Dave led the first half as a single running belay. Annette led all the way to an area referred to as the "Tarzan Leap." Todd and Ken followed, climbing from fixed belays and alternating leads.

Dave, Annette, and Dan summited at 12:30 p.m. They spent only about five minutes on the summit due to threatening weather. About three pitches below the summit, nearing a chimney pitch, Todd was leading a short traverse followed by a steep vertical section. He was able to place two pieces of protection in the traverse. (He recalls that the vertical section did not offer many places for protection.) He stopped to place protection at an awkward stance just below the nest ledge. His left arm was levered in a crack and there was only a shaky right hand hold. He was reaching with his right hand for a piece of protection when he fell about 25–30 feet, bouncing off one ledge and ending up on his back on a larger ledge.

Ken estimated that Todd was unconscious for about five minutes. Todd was then able to crawl to Ken's belay station where Ken anchored him and then signaled the other team members with a whistle.

Dan arrived first and did a quick medical assessment. He determined that Todd had several fractured ribs and that his breathing was extremely labored and painful. Todd's right arm and hand were not functioning properly, and he complained of lower back pain. Ken was able to communicate with some climbers below, who promptly went down for help. (By this time, the weather had turned, and it proceeded to rain and hail for the next six hours.) To get down to a larger ledge, Todd was able to rappel slowly with assistance. The team continued to rappel, as this seemed to be the quickest and safest means to reach the notch at the top of the gullies. In the meantime, a helicopter had dropped off a paramedic on the snowfield 150 feet below the ridge. The team set up a double rope rappel all the way to the snow. Todd was then assisted across some relatively steep snow slopes to a level area where the helicopter was able to pick him up. He was flown directly to Twisp, where they landed for a brief period of time to warm him up and administer first aid. He was then flown to Central Washington Hospital, where his diagnoses included a compressed fracture of L1, two broken ribs, and an injured right arm and hand.

Analysis

The fact that the particular section of the route is not easy to protect combined with the moderate experience level of the victim contributed to the incident. Also, the initial approach on this pitch is deceptively easy.

The team was able to accomplish a self rescue off the most difficult part of the route under adverse conditions. This was due to a very well organized and efficient team effort when things *really* counted. (Source: From a report submitted by Todd Campbell.)

FALL ON SNOW – FAULTY USE OF CRAMPONS
Washington, North Cascades National Park, Mount Shuksan

On September 19, a group of six Seattle Mountaineers were descending the "Winnie's Slide" section of the Fisher Chimney route on Mount Shuksan when one member fell and arrested within ten feet. However, he was unable to move. He said he had heard and felt a "snap" when he fell.

He was rescued by helicopter and flown to a hospital. He had fractured his fibula.

Analysis

The victim said that part of the group had chosen not to use crampons, but that he was wearing them, and that it was quite possible that the snow build up in them contributed to his fall. (Source: From a report written by Kelly Bush, Ranger at NCNP)

(There were several other reports from North Cascades National Park that did not get entered into the data. These included five overdue climbers, one of whom, though uninjured, took a helicopter ride. Two hikers got into climbing situations and wound up falling. One fellow who deliberately went off trail on Cascade Pass realized that he had made a "foolish choice" when he jumped off a rock bluff in a mixed snow and rock area. He fractured his ankle.)

MISSING CLIMBERS, SEVERE WEATHER
Washington, Mount Rainier, Muir Snowfield

Chris Hartonas (40) and Raymond Vakili (48) disappeared while climbing to Camp Muir on November 5. Hartonas and Vakili were experienced mountaineers and both men had been to Camp Muir before. Hartonas was an avid park visitor and mountain climber, known by many on the Park Service staff for his frequent ascents to Camp Muir, particularly under adverse weather conditions.

An extensive ten-day search ensued. Park Rangers, Rainier Mountaineering Guides, Volunteer Mountain Rescue, friends of the men, and search dog teams participated. Severe weather that included heavy snowfall and rain, high winds and whiteouts hampered efforts throughout much of the operation. US Army Reserve and private helicopters supported ground teams with aerial reconnaissance during periods of clear weather. The search was concluded on November 16 with no clues of the two climbers found.

Analysis

This was the fourth serious incident on the Muir Snowfield in 1999. Without clues, it's difficult to speculate what exactly happened to the men. It's perplexing when two experienced, cautious and mature climbers just disappear. They were well equipped and Hartonas was very familiar with the area. Both men have a history of good decision making in the mountains and neither had a reputation for "pushing it." (Source: Mike Gauthier, SAR Ranger, Mount Ranier National Park)

FALL ON ICE, NO PROTECTION OR BELAY
Washington, Mount Rainier, Cowlitz Cleaver

While searching for missing climbers Chris Hartonas and Raymond Vakili on November 15, three rescuers sustained serious injuries after falling off the Gibraltar Ledges route. Park Ranger Asha Anderson and Rainier Mountaineering Guides Ashley Garmin and Art Rausch were searching along the Cowlitz Cleaver when the accident occurred. The rope team of three was part of a five person search team looking for clues along the route Hartonas and Vakili may have attempted to ascend. Anderson had just joined Garmin and Rausch on their climbing rope to cross an exposed icy gully at 10,400 feet. While traversing the chute, Anderson lost her footing and fell, pulling Garmin and Rausch despite everyone's aggressive efforts to self arrest. The team of three slid and tumbled uncontested down the 45-degree water ice slope for nearly 600 feet before coming to a rest on the upper Muir Snowfield near 9,900 feet. Search team leader Joe Puryear witnessed the accident and radioed for emergency assistance as the trio slid out of sight.

Another field search team was quickly dispatched to an emergency landing zone where a Chinook Helicopter, also doing aerial search, picked them up. That team, along with another aerial reconnaissance team in a smaller helicopter, was reinserted near the accident site. Together, they provided a very rapid rescue, airlifting the injured searchers off the mountain. During the fall, Anderson had sustained two broken ankles and ribs; Garmin had head lacerations and a broken back, while Rausch escaped with only a broken rib. All were seriously sore and bruised.

Analysis

Conditions on the mountain were unique at the time. Hard, thick water ice covered everything between 8000 and 12,000 feet. It was as though a glass of water had been poured on the mountain and allowed to freeze.

Puryear's team searched the Camp Muir area first, then began a searching ascent of the Cowlitz Cleaver towards the "Beehive." At the time, Garmin and Rausch roped up because they would be searching along the edge of the glacier while Anderson, Puryear and S. Richards remained unroped, searching along the fourth-class cleaver. The team reconvened near 10,400 feet to cross a steep gully. Puryear and Richards successfully crossed the chute first. During that time, Rausch noticed that Anderson was concerned about the situation. He offered to have her join his rope team, which she did. Then they continued across the chute. Anderson could not recall what caused the slip, but once the slide started, it proved impossible to stop. Garmin and Rausch felt they could provide a team self arrest, but the ice proved too hard and their axes bounced off. As the team tumbled faster, everyone believed that, "this is it."

Rausch observantly noted Anderson's apprehension. Better communication amongst the entire team about each individual's skills and the terrain hazards may have lead to the decision to belay or place snow/ice protection along the route. (Source: Mike Gauthier, SAR Ranger, Mount Ranier National Park)

(Editor's Note: Mike Gauthier points out that if Mount Rainier had a Bermuda Triangle, the route to Camp Muir would be it. This popular climb on a clear day is

straightforward and benign, but in poor weather, it has many hazards, most particularly cliffs and crevasses that mark its perimeter. The Park spent over $150,000 on mountain related search, rescue and recovery in 1999. Many of these costs were related to extensive searches for lost mountaineers on the route to Camp Muir, the mountain's most popular high camp.

In Olympic National Park, there was one incident that was mountain related. A hiker (31) from the Netherlands was found after an extensive search. He was located at the base of a very steep snow slope a quarter mile east of the Glacier Meadows Ranger station. Footprints indicated that he was going to climb to the ridge to gain a photo opportunity. But the terrain was technical—a steep chute filled with snow. As this search and recovery cost $56,000, it is mentioned here because the media often refer to incidents like this as "climbing" accidents.)

AVALANCHE, POOR POSITION – KNOWN AVALANCHE HAZARD
Wyoming, Grand Teton National Park, Mount Teewinot

On May 23 at 1300, Jackson climber Phillip Jones arrived at the Jenny Lake Ranger Station to report that his climbing partner, Irene McManus, had been swept 2,000 feet down the East Face of Mount Teewinot by an avalanche. According to Jones, McManus sustained serious injuries in the fall. Jones said he descended to McManus' position at the toe of the avalanche, removed her from the debris pile, and placed her on a rock on the north side of the slide path. She was reported to be conscious but in significant pain, with head trauma and possible fractures to the back, shoulder and ribs.

As rescue coordinator for the day, I requested that the park contract helicopter and pilot Ken Johnson be dispatched to the Lupine Meadows Rescue Cache. The helicopter arrived at 1340. With Ranger Renny Jackson serving as spotter, Randy Benham, George Montopoli, Leo Larson, Chris Harder, Jack McConnell, and Dave Bywater were inserted via short haul directly to the scene. Harder was positioned on the northwest side of the Apex to serve as avalanche guard, as additional avalanche activity continued throughout the afternoon.

Following full patient stabilization, McManus was immobilized on a backboard inside a litter and short hauled directly to Lupine Meadows Heli base with Ranger Montopoli attending. McManus was transferred to a Teton County Ambulance and taken to St. John's Hospital where she was admitted with multiple trauma.

Due to ongoing, hazardous avalanche activity, all field rescue personnel were then extracted from the scene via helicopter short haul.

Analysis

According to Phillip Jones, he and McManus had spent the night of May 22 on the top of the Apex, with plans to climb the East Face route the following morning. Jones said they observed avalanche activity on the face during the afternoon of the 22nd, so they planned an early morning climb.

They left their campsite around 0400 on the 23rd and climbed the East Face route as planned. Jones described the conditions as good, with firm snow. They wore crampons to the summit, arriving around 0910. After about 45 minutes to an hour, they began their descent. Jones said they were just clearing the lower end of the narrows when he observed a large volume of wet snow and water release from above. He was about 30 to 40 yards below McManus and out of the slide track. He watched McManus plant her ice ax, but the fast moving, airborne slide knocked her off her feet. Jones said that McManus tumbled and cartwheeled past him as the slide carried her about 2,000 feet down the face.

Jones descended to McManus' position at the toe of the slide. McManus was conscious but in significant pain. She told Jones that she had been partially buried in the debris pile but was able to dig herself out.

In a follow up telephone interview with McManus on May 24, she offered the same account of the incident as described above and said the ride down the slide path was extremely violent. Her crampons were torn from her boots, ski poles torn from her pack, and other items of equipment lost. McManus confirmed that she was partially buried in the debris pile and had been able to thrust one arm and one leg out of the slide as she came to rest. She said this allowed her to dig herself out. She also said she struggled with her pack pulling her down while sliding in the debris, and with snow filling her airway.

Both Jones and McManus were wearing crampons, helmet, avalanche transceiver, and were using their ice axes at the time of the slide. McManus has been climbing for four years and Jones one year, and both had climbed the East Face of Teewinot early last summer. (Source: Mark Magnuson, SAR Coordinator)

FALL ON SNOW, UNABLE TO SELF ARREST, EXCEEDING ABILITIES
Wyoming, Grand Teton National Park, Mount Moran

Joseph Boots Allen, Justin Watsabaugh and Micha Thompson left a camp in a snow cave near the base of the Skillet Glacier on Mount Moran (12,605 feet) on June 20 at 0230. They climbed the glacier at night and reached the summit some time between 0530 and 0630. About 0700 the three began a ski descent of the Skillet Glacier. Allen was the last to descend and as he neared the bottom of the "handle" on the skillet, he fell. This was 500 to 1,000 feet below the summit. He attributes this to hitting some ice or slush on the surface of the snow, which caused him to lose control of his skis. Allen attempted to perform a self arrest with his ice ax, but this was unsuccessful. He slid into a runnel and then down the length of the glacier. In the process he slid over a rock outcropping known as "Rock Island" and then came to rest in avalanche debris. Allen fell a distance of 2,000 to 2,500 feet before stopping. His companions descended to his location and then provided medical care before moving him from the avalanche hazard. Watsabaugh descended to report the accident while Thompson stayed with the patient.

Analysis

Allen was admitted to Saint John's Hospital in Jackson with a dislocated hip and numerous abrasions. He had first skied at the age of three, but admitted that this was more difficult than anything he had attempted. The skiing party started very early in the morning to avoid any avalanche hazard. Allen was wearing a helmet, which probably saved him from serious injury or death. Allen's companions took appropriate actions to treat his injuries and remove him from the avalanche danger. These factors combined to reduce the severity of this accident. (Source: Rick Perch, SAR Ranger)

(Editor's Note: As reported in previous editions of ANAM, the Skillet Glacier has seen many accidents, especially on descents.)

LIGHTNING
Wyoming, Grand Teton National Park, Grand Teton

Around 1130 on August 5, Ranger Janet Wilts and Chris Goodhue were struck by lightning at the top of the Friction Pitch of the Exum Ridge on the Grand Teton. (Jan Cauthorn Page, the third member of the team, was not struck.) Wilts reported that the lightning entered her right elbow, traveled down her arm, and exited her right thumb and forefinger, with accompanying numbness, tingling, and weakness. Goodhue reported that the lightning entered her buttocks, traveled down her right leg, and exited her middle toe, leaving a small exit wound, with accompanying numbness, tingling, and weakness. Wilts reported that she felt the party would be able to traverse off the mountain once the storm had passed, and spoke with Ranger Tom Kimbrough, who was in the vicinity of the Eye of the Needle with two climbing partners.

Kimbrough began ascending toward the Upper Saddle to assist Wilts, while medical control was contacted. The decision was made to have them traverse off the mountain as soon as possible, descend to the Lower Saddle, and be transported to Lupine Meadows by helicopter.

About 1545, Wilts, Kimbrough, and parties, arrived at the Lower Saddle. The contract helicopter, with heli-tack personnel S. Markason (USFS), was diverted from an on going rescue on Teewinot Mountain to pick up Wilts and Goodhue. They arrived Lupine Meadows at 1615 where they self transported to Saint John's Hospital for medical evaluation. (Source: George Montopoli, SAR Ranger)

(Editor's Note: While lightning is not uncommon in this range, it is less common in the mornings. The Exum Ridge is a particularly exposed place. Many climbers have experienced hits and near misses from lightning while descending the Owen-Spalding.)

FALL ON SNOW, LOSS OF CONTROL – VOLUNTARY GLISSADE, FAULTY USE OF CRAMPONS, INEXPERIENCE
Wyoming, Grand Teton National Park, Mount Teewinot

On the morning of July 17, David Berry and Andrew Baldyga departed Yellowstone National Park and stopped at Jenny Lake Ranger Station to obtain climbing information on Teewinot's East Face route. Ranger Randy Benham recalls talking briefly to Berry and Baldyga about conditions on this route. He told them about the lingering snow on the East Face route and the need to cross the large snowfield in the middle of the face. Benham also mentioned the "tricky" fourth-class rock section above this snowfall. He does not remember any other particulars about this contact. Since day climbs do not require registration, most of these contacts at Jenny Lake Ranger Station are brief in duration. Berry and Baldyga then drove toward Moose and Jackson where they visited several mountain shops, purchased some gear, rented crampons and bought some food. They drove back later that evening and camped at Lupine Meadows Trailhead, retiring for the evening at 2345.

At 0920 the next morning, they awoke, ate breakfast, and then started their ascent at 1000. According to Berry, they climbed until approximately 1630 where they waited out a short-duration snow squall and tried to find a line of ascent through the fourth-class rock crux above. Unable to pass through this section with confidence and with the hour getting late, the duo began their descent at 1800. Berry led the way until he encountered the large snowfield that lies in the middle of Teewinot's East Face. Berry decided to descend on rock, while Baldyga opted for a snow descent. Berry continued down on rock for around 200 feet before gaining access to the large snowfield. Both climbers stopped to affix crampons, made the transition to snow and continued down slowly with Berry slightly ahead of Baldyga. After descending a short distance, Berry stopped to wait for Baldyga. Berry heard a noise above and looked up to see Baldyga cartwheeling down the snowfield. Baldyga's fall, estimated at 600 feet, took him out of view of Berry. Berry cautiously continued down to try to locate his climbing partner. Baldyga came to rest a short distance from three other climbers (O'Connor, Ruthardt and Sherwood) who moved him a short distance to a large down-sloping ledge, administered first aid and dialed 911 on their cell phone at 1917.

Ranger Larson received notice of the accident through Teton Dispatch and requested a contract helicopter. Helicopter 43T, piloted by Ken Johnson, arrived at Lupine Meadows at 1958. Spotter Perch, along with Rangers Byerly and Johnson, conducted a reconnaissance flight of the accident scene, which had previously been located via a spotting scope and verbal guidance from Sherwood. The helicopter returned to Lupine Meadows and was rigged for a short haul mission. With Perch as spotter, Byerly and Johnson were inserted to the accident site, followed by Benham and Jernigan on the subsequent flight. No pulse or respirations were detected, and given the massive trauma present, a DNR order was given at 2032. The body of Baldyga was long lined from the accident scene to Lupine Meadows at 2120 and released, along with personal property, to County Coroner Bob Campbell.

Analysis

Teewinot, highly visible from the much traveled east side of the Teton Range, is one of the most important Teton peaks in terms of placement, size, and popularity. In a *Climber's Guide to the Teton Range* by Leigh Ortenburger and Reynold Jackson, the authors state, "The routes on the East Face can be studied at length from the highway with binoculars or telescope. The ascent of Teewinot, however, should be taken seriously because the moderately steep snow in the East Face couloir has been the site of several accidents. Knowledge of use of the ice ax is essential for early and midseason climbs." Given the heavy snow load of 1999, a mid-July ascent definitely would require knowledge of moderate snow travel.

The East Face of Teewinot Mountain is a long (5,600 feet of elevation) climb requiring approximately six and a half to eight hours to ascend from Lupine Meadows. An alpine start is desirable to reach the summit before the customary afternoon thunderstorms roll through.

Andrew Baldyga and David Berry were intimidated at the thought of downclimbing the main East Face snowfield. Berry stayed on rock as long as possible before gaining the snowfield, while Baldyga opted to access the snow tongues above the main snowfield. Both climbers stopped to attach crampons, even though the snow was moderately soft at 2100, according to SAR rangers on scene who felt comfortable without crampons during their descent of the main snowfield at 2200. Baldyga and Berry descended the main snowfield slowly. Berry fell a couple of times but was able to self arrest after a short distance.

Andrew Baldyga was last seen by witnesses butt glissading feet first with ice ax in hand. He did not appear to be attempting self arrest, gained speed, and probably caught a crampon, which sent him cartwheeling out of control. He fell approximately 600 feet before coming to rest near a large down-sloping ledge. His ice ax (a nine-ounce Grivel with no wristband attached) was located 100 feet above him and his crampons were still firmly attached to his lightweight boots.

One can only speculate why Baldyga did not attempt to self arrest immediately. His inexperience on snow might have made self arrest a time consuming, conscious act, allowing too much speed to accumulate and panic to set in. Perhaps Baldyga did not realize the gravity of the situation and the need for immediate self-arrest attempts. Perhaps he was thinking a butt glissade was a great way to descend. (Source: Leo Larson, SAR Ranger)

(Editor's Note: There was another accident on the East Face route involving a fall on snow near an area known as The Idol and Worshiper. John Pagendarm, who was climbing alone, lost his self arrest position and fell head first into a moat. Thanks to other climbers nearby, a ranger team and contract helicopter were able to extricate him within a few hours. He suffered a basal skull fracture and several facial fractures.

Other mountain related incidents in the Tetons included two cases of acute mountain sickness [AMS], one to a hiker and one to a guided client on the Grand Teton; one severe knee injury from a fall while skiing down from the Lower Saddle; and one femur fracture resulting when a snow boarder hit a rock at the bottom of a fifty-foot jump he took in a remote area known as "Unskiabowl." The latter two required helicopter evacuation. The question is whether to call these "mountaineering" accidents. Neither party, unlike the Steve Koch climb and snowboard descent of Mount Owen last year, set out to engage in any form of climbing or ski—now to include snowboard—mountaineering.

It may be a fine line, but in any case, it certainly complicates the editing job! At least the readers—and who knows, maybe even potential victims—are made aware of complications that are set in motion when serious injuries happen in back country ski accidents.)

TABLE I
REPORTED MOUNTAINEERING ACCIDENTS

	Number of Accidents Reported		Total Persons Involved		Injured		Fatalities	
	USA	CAN	USA	CAN	USA	CAN	USA	CAN
1951	15		22		11		3	
1952	31		35		17		13	
1953	24		27		12		12	
1954	31		41		31		8	
1955	34		39		28		6	
1956	46		72		54		13	
1957	45		53		28		18	
1958	32		39		23		11	
1959	42	2	56	2	31	0	19	2
1960	47	4	64	12	37	8	19	4
1961	49	9	61	14	45	10	14	4
1962	71	1	90	1	64	0	19	1
1963	68	11	79	12	47	10	19	2
1964	53	11	65	16	44	10	14	3
1965	72	0	90	0	59	0	21	0
1966	67	7	80	9	52	6	16	3
1967	74	10	110	14	63	7	33	5
1968	70	13	87	19	43	12	27	5
1969	94	11	125	17	66	9	29	2
1970	129	11	174	11	88	5	15	5
1971	110	17	138	29	76	11	31	7
1972	141	29	184	42	98	17	49	13
1973	108	6	131	6	85	4	36	2
1974	96	7	177	50	75	1	26	5
1975	78	7	158	22	66	8	19	2
1976	137	16	303	31	210	9	53	6
1977	121	30	277	49	106	21	32	11
1978	118	17	221	19	85	6	42	10
1979	100	36	137	54	83	17	40	19
1980	191	29	295	85	124	26	33	8
1981	97	43	223	119	80	39	39	6
1982	140	48	305	126	120	43	24	14
1983	187	29	442	76	169	26	37	7
1984	182	26	459	63	174	15	26	6
1985	195	27	403	62	190	22	17	3
1986	203	31	406	80	182	25	37	14
1987	192	25	377	79	140	23	32	9
1988	156	18	288	44	155	18	24	4
1989	141	18	272	36	124	11	17	9
1990	136	25	245	50	125	24	24	4
1991	169	20	302	66	147	11	18	6
1992	175	17	351	45	144	11	43	6
1993	132	27	274	50	121	17	21	14

	Number of Accidents Reported		Total Persons Involved		Injured		Fatalities	
	USA	CAN	USA	CAN	USA	CAN	USA	CAN
1994	158	25	335	58	131	25	27	5
1995	168	24	353	50	134	18	37	7
1996	139	28	261	59	100	16	31	6
1997	158	35	323	87	148	24	31	13
1998	138	24	281	55	138	18	20	1
1999	122	29	245	69	91	20	16	10
Totals	5074	755	9227	1603	4331	599	1194	259

TABLE II

Geographical Districts	1951–1998			1999		
	Number of Accidents	Deaths	Total Persons Involved	Number of Accidents	Deaths	Total Persons Involved
Canada						
Alberta	396	113	870	20	7	50
British Columbia	264	103	588	7	2	16
Yukon Territory	33	26	73	0	0	0
Ontario	33	8	61	2	1	3
Quebec	27	7	58	0	0	0
East Arctic	7	2	20	0	0	0
West Arctic	1	1	2	0	0	0
Practice Cliffs[1]	20	2	36	0	0	0
United States						
Alaska	397	157	622	16	3	26
Arizona, Nevada Texas	73	13	138	0	0	0
Atlantic–North	737	100	1248	31	2	54
Atlantic–South	70	21	133	4	0	7
California	995	236	2070	27	2	52
Central[2]	121	13	194	1	1	2
Colorado	641	188	1106	9	0	21
Montana, Idaho South Dakota	64	25	98	6	0	11
Oregon	144	71	343	5	2	19
Utah, New Mexico	117	40	211	3	1	5
Washington	934	274	689	13	4	31
Wyoming	483	106	887	7	1	17

[1]This category includes bouldering, as well as artificial climbing walls, buildings, and so forth. These are also added to the count of each state and province, but not to the total count, though that error has been made in previous years. Also, the Practice Cliffs category has been removed from the U.S. data.

(Editor's Note: The totoal reported for the category Injured in Table I above for 1998 was 281. It should have been recorded as 138 and the Total for 1998 should read 4234.)

TABLE III

	1951–98 USA	1959–98 CAN.	1999 USA	1999 CAN.
Terrain				
Rock	3674	445	84	10
Snow	2109	313	29	11
Ice	198	104	9	8
River	13	3	0	0
Unknown	22	8	0	0
Ascent or Descent				
Ascent	3258	469	87	14
Descent	1987	323	35	14
Unknown	247	4	0	1
Immediate Cause				
Fall or slip on rock	2548	239	62	7
Slip on snow or ice	828	166	16	5
Falling rock, ice, or object	506	114	17	4
Exceeding abilities	440	27	13	1
Avalanche	260	109	2	2
Exposure	241	13	0	0
Illness[1]	287	21	13	1
Stranded	275	11	5	0
Rappel Failure/Error	221	40	6	0
Loss of control/glissade	169	16	2	0
Fall into crevasse/moat	136	41	5	3
Failure to follow route	131	27	3	1
Nut/chock pulled out	110	3	14	1
Piton/ice screw pulled out	86	12	1	0
Faulty use of crampons	70	5	4	0
Lightning	39	7	1	0
Skiing	48	9	2	0
Ascending too fast	45	0	1	0
Equipment failure	11	2	0	0
Other[2]	229	28	40	4
Unknown	60	8	0	0
Contributory Causes				
Climbing unroped	912	151	7	2
Exceeding abilities	838	184	9	10
Inadequate equipment/clothing	559	72	8	3
Placed no/inadequate protection	530	79	22	0
Weather	388	57	12	1
Climbing alone	329	57	9	3
No hard hat	260	25	9	3
Nut/chock pulled out	185	16	4	1
Darkness	122	19	1	0
Party separated	103	17	2	0
Poor position	121	15	5	0
Inadequate belay	135	22	9	0
Piton/ice screw pulled out	84	10	0	0

	1951–98 USA	1959–98 CAN.	1999 USA	1999 CAN.
Contributory Causes (cont.)				
Failure to test holds	75	18	5	1
Exposure	55	13	1	0
Failed to follow directions	62	8	6	3
Illness[1]	32	4	1	0
Equipment failure	10	6	0	1
Other[2]	238	79	1	6
Age of Individuals				
Under 15	117	12	0	0
15-20	1166	197	9	2
21-25	1180	225	19	11
26-30	1075	189	20	4
31-35	718	96	21	6
36-50	904	108	33	16
Over 50	148	20	6	2
Unknown	954	596	45	26
Experience Level				
None/Little	1543	280	11	11
Moderate (1 to 3 years)	1369	340	17	6
Experienced	1449	359	61	12
Unknown	1574	403	55	40
Month of Year				
January	193	15	0	1
February	182	40	2	1
March	252	52	4	3
April	344	29	5	0
May	739	49	23	1
June	881	59	31	0
July	952	225	10	5
August	887	143	18	12
September	1077	54	8	4
October	353	30	11	0
November	160	10	6	0
December	71	17	4	2
Unknown	12	1	0	0
Type of Injury/Illness (Data since 1984)				
Fracture	825	155	50	10
Laceration	447	58	29	1
Abrasion	233	40	7	2
Bruise	274	63	29	1
Sprain/strain	204	21	11	2
Concussion	150	14	13	6
Hypothermia	121	12	6	1

	1951–98 USA	1959–98 CAN.	1999 USA	1999 CAN.
Type of Injury/Illness (cont.)				
Frostbite	88	8	5	1
Dislocation	75	9	7	1
Puncture	30	5	0	3
Acute Mountain Sickness	21	0	2	0
HAPE	51	0	1	0
HACE	17	0	2	0
Other[3]	200	33	10	2
None	134	73	7	3

[1]These illnesses/injuries, which led directly to the incident, included: fatigue (6), dehydration (8), snow-blindness, exhaustion (2), HACE (2), HAPE, collapsed lung, pneumothorax, appendicitis, and concussion.

[2]These included, among others: unable to self-arrest (8), hand hold or foothold broke off (9), dislodged rock severed climbing rope, "snagged" crampons (4), inadequate food/water (3), failed to turn back, rope "unclipped" from carabiner, did not check to see that fixed rope reached the destination, forgot to finish tie-in knot, dropped pack with needed protection in it, disappeared (Muir Snowfield), new rock climbing shoes - slipped on wet rock (2), cornice failure, whiteout (4), poor rope handling (4), white-out (6).

[3]These included: pneumothorax, snow blindness, collapsed lungs (3), dehydration (8), punctured lung, fatigue (6), exhaustion (2), rope burn (2), and appendicitis.

(Editor's Note: Under the category "other," many of the particular items will have been recorded under a general category. For example, the climber who dislodges a rock that falls on another climber would be coded as Falling Rock/Object, or the climber who has a hand hold come loose and falls would also be coded as Fall On Rock.

In the category "Other" for the U.S. last year, Table III reported 86. This should have read 26. Totals have been corrected.)

Mountain Rescue Units in North America
**Denotes team fully certified—Technical Rock,
Snow & Ice, Wilderness Search;
S, R, SI = certified partially in Search, Rock, and/or Snow & Ice

ALASKA
Alaska Mtn. Rescue Group. POB 241102, Anchorage, AK 99524
resqr@alaska.net. www.amrg.org
Denali National Park SAR. Talkeetna, AK   Dena_talkeetna@nps.gov
US Army Alaskan Warfare Training Center. Alaska

ARIZONA
Apache Rescue Team. POB 107, Nutrioso, AZ 95932
Arizona Department of Public Safety Air Rescue. Phoenix, Flagstaff, Tucson,
Kingman, AZ
Arizona Division of Emergency Services. Phoenix, AZ
Grand Canyon National Park Rescue Team. POB 129, Grand Canyon,
AZ 86023
****Central Arizona Mountain Rescue Assn/Maricopa County Sheriff's Office
MR.** POB 4004 Phoenix, AZ 85030-4004   CAMRA@aztec.asu.edu.com
Sedona Fire District Special Operations Rescue Team. 2860 Southwest Dr.,
Sedona, AZ 86336   ropes@sedona.net
****Southern Arizona Rescue Assn / Pima County Sheriff's Office.** POB 12892,
Tucson, AZ 85732-2892

CALIFORNIA
****Altadena Mountain Rescue Team.** 780 E. Altadena Dr., Altadena, CA 91001
www.hsc.usc.edu
****Bay Area Mountain Rescue Team.** POB 6384, Stanford, CA 94309
bamru@hooked.net
California Office of Emergency Services. Sacramento, CA
warning.center@oes.ca.gov
****China Lake Mountain Rescue Group.** POB 2037, Ridgecrest, CA 93556
tsakai@ridgecrest.ca.us   www.clmrg.org
****Inyo County Sheriff's Posse SAR.** 3522 Brookside Drive; Bishop, CA 93514
gscorliss@qnet.com
Joshua Tree National Park SAR. Twenty Nine Palms, CA
patrick_suddath@nps.gov
****Los Padres SAR Team.** POB 6602, Santa Barbara, CA 93160-6602
****Malibu Mountain Rescue Team.** POB 222, Malibu, CA 90265,
73020.3021.RLebrun@gte.net
****Montrose Sar Team.** POB 404, Montrose, CA 91021   lynjerry@aol.com
****Riverside Mountain Rescue Unit.** POB 5444, Riverside, CA 92517
bryant@cyberg8+.com
San Bernardino County Sheriff's Cave Rescue Team. 655 E. Third St.
San Bernardino, CA 92415-0061   blavender@sanbernardinosheriff.org
****San Bernardino County SO/West Valley SAR.** 627 Aspen Way, Upland,
CA 91786   boobali@gte.net

San Diego Mountain Rescue Team. POB 81602, San Diego, CA 92138
    mbell@newwaypro.com
San Dimas Mountain Rescue Team. POB 35, San Dimas, CA 91773
    wdland@linkline.com
Santa Clarita Valley SAR / L.A.S.O. 23740 Magic Mountain Parkway, Valencia,
    CA 91355
Sequoia-Kings Canyon National Park Rescue Team. Three Rivers, CA 93271
Sierra Madre SAR. POB 24, Sierra Madre, CA 91025   BURHENTA@sce.com
Ventura County SAR. 2101 E. Olson Rd, Thousand Oaks, CA 91362
    www.ventura.org/sheriff/vip.htm#b
Yosemite National Park Rescue Team. POB 577-SAR, Yosemite National Park,
    CA 95389

COLORADO
Alpine Rescue Team. POB 934, Evergreen, CO 80439
    Alpinerescueteam@juno.com
Colorado Ground SAR. 2391 Ash St, Denver, CO 80222
Crested Butte SAR. POB 485, Crested Butte, CO 81224
El Paso County SAR. 3950 Interpark Dr, Colorado Springs, CO 80907-9028
Eldorado Canyon State Park. POB B, Eldorado Springs, CO 80025
Grand County SAR. Box 172, Winter Park, CO 80482
Larimer County SAR. POB 1271, Fort Collins, CO 80522-0106
    lcsar@co.larimer.co.us
Mountain Rescue Aspen. 630 W. Main St, Aspen, CO 81611
Park County SAR, CO. POB 721, Fairplay, CO 80440
    dthorson@compuserve.com
Rocky Mountain National Park Rescue Team. Estes Park, CO 80517
Rocky Mountain Rescue Group. POB Y, Boulder, CO 80306   rmrg@csn.org
Routt County SAR. 911 Yampa Ave/ POB 772837, Steamboat Springs, CO 80477
Summit County Rescue Group. POB 1794, Breckenridge, CO 80424
Vail Mountain Rescue Group. POB 1597, Vail, CO 81658   vmrg@vail.net
Western State College Mountain Rescue Team. Western State College Union,
    Gunnison, CO 81231   org_mrt@western.edu

IDAHO
Bonneville County SAR. 605 N. Capital Ave, Idaho Falls, ID 83402   stf@inel.gov
Idaho Mountain SAR. POB 741, Boise, ID 83701   IDSAR@execu.net

MAINE
Acadia National Park SAR. Bar Harbor, ME

MARYLAND
Maryland SAR Group. 5434 Vantage Point Road, Columbia, MD 21044
    Peter_McCabe@Ed.gov

MONTANA
Glacier National Park SAR. POB 423, Glacier National Park, West Glacier,
    MT 59936

Northwest Montana Regional SAR Assn. c/o Flat County SO, 800 S. Main, Kalispell, MT 59901
**Western Montana Mountain Rescue Team. University of Montana, University Center – Rm 105, Missoula, MT 59812

NEVADA
**Las Vegas Metro PD SAR. 2990 N. Rancho, Las Vegas, NV 89130
   clintsar@ix.netcom.com   http://intermind.net/~speleo/index.html

NEW HAMPSHIRE
Appalachian Mountain Club. Pinkham Notch Camp, Gorham, NH 03581
Mountain Rescue Service. PO Box 494, North Conway, NH 03860

NEW MEXICO
**Albuquerque Mountain Rescue Council. POB 53396, Albuquerque, NM 87153
   albrescu@swcp.com

NEW YORK
76 SAR. Box 876, Guilderland, NY 12084-0876   adkxs@aol.com
NY State Forest Rangers. Albany, NY

OREGON
**Corvallis Mountain Rescue Unit. POB 116, Corvallis, OR 97339
(S,R) Deschutes County MR. 63333 West Highway 20 Bend, OR 97701
   Moles@transport.com
**Eugene Mountain Rescue. POB 10081, Eugene, OR 97401
**Hood River Crag Rats Rescue Team. 2126 Tucker Rd, Hood River, OR 97031
**Portland Mountain Rescue. POB 5391, Portland, OR 97228   rockyh9@idt.net

PENNSYLVANIA
**Allegheny Mountain Rescue Group. c/o Mercy Hospital, 1400 Locust, Pittsburgh, PA 15219-5166   vmiller@nb.net
**Wilderness Emergency Strike Team. 11 North Duke Street, Lancaster, PA 17602   rsadd@redrose.net   www.redrose.net

UTAH
**Davis County Sheriff's SAR. POB 618, Farmington, UT 84025
   jakeh@co.davis.ut.us
Rocky Mountain Rescue Dogs. 3353 S. Main #122, Salt Lake City, UT 84115
**Salt Lake County Sheriff's SAR. 3473 E. 7590 S., Salt Lake City, UT 84121
San Juan County Emergency Services. POB 9, Monticello, UT 84539
**Utah County Sherrif's SAR. POB 330, Provo, UT 84603-0330
   ucsar@utah.uswest.net
**Weber County Sheriff's Mountain Rescue. 745 Nancy Dr, Ogden, UT 84403
Zion National Park SAR. Springdale, UT 84767

VERMONT
Stowe Hazardous Terrain Evacuation. P.O. Box 291, Stowe, VT 05672
neilvand@aol.com

VIRGINIA
Air Force Rescue Coordination Center. Suite 101, 205 Dodd Boulevard,
Langley AFB, VA 23665-2789   airforce.rescue@usa.net   www.afrcc.org

WASHINGTON STATE
Bellingham Mountain Rescue Council. POB 292, Bellingham, WA 98227
Central Washington Mountain Rescue. POB 2663, Yakima, WA 98907
Everett Mountain Rescue Unit. POB 2566, Everett, WA 98203
Mount Rainier National Park Rescue Team. Longmire, WA 98397
North Cascades National Park Rescue Team. 728 Ranger Station Rd,
Marblemount, WA 98267
Olympic Mountain Rescue. POB 4244, Bremerton, WA 98312
rogerrescu@aol.com
Olympic National Park Rescue Team. 600 Park Ave, Port Angeles, WA 98362
Seattle Mountain Rescue. POB 67, Seattle, WA 98111
Skagit Mountain Rescue. POB 2, Mt. Vernon, WA 98273
Tacoma Mountain Rescue. POB 696, Tacoma, WA 98401
Volcano Rescue Team. 404 S. Parcel Ave, Yacolt, WA 98675

WASHINGTON, D.C.
National Park Service, EMS/SAR Division. Washington, D.C.
US Park Police Aviation. Washington, D.C.

WYOMING
Grand Teton National Park Rescue Team. POB 67, Moose, WY 83012
Park County SAR, WY. Park County SO, 1131 11th, Cody, WY 82412

CANADA
North Shore Rescue Team. 165 E. 13th St, North Vancouver, B.C.,
Canada V7L 2L3
Rocky Mountain House SAR. Bag 5000, RCMP, Rocky Mountain House,
Alta, Canada T0M 1T0

MOUNTAIN RESCUE ASSOCIATION
710 Tenth Street, #105
Golden, CO 80401
Phone: 602-205-4066 • Fax: 602-973-0166
Internet: www.mra.org • email: mra@mra.org

Tim Kovacs, President
Maricopa County Mountain Rescue/Central Arizona MRA, AZ
tkovacs@goodnet.com

Rocky Henderson, Vice President
Portland Mountain Rescue, OR
rockyh9@idt.net

Tom Frazer, Secretary/Treasurer
El Paso County SAR, CO
tfrazer@earthlink.net

Monty Bell, Member at Large
San Diego MRT, CA
mbell@newwaypro.com

Rod Knopp, Member at Large
Idaho Mountain Search and Rescue, ID
rsksearch@aol.com